lebanese home cooking

Simple, Delicious, Mostly Vegetarian Recipes from the Founder of Beirut's Souk el Tayeb Market

Kamal Mouzawak

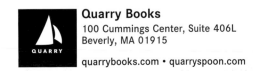

Quarry Books
100 Cummings Center, Suite 406L
Beverly, MA 01915

quarrybooks.com • quarryspoon.com

First published in the United States of America in 2015 by
Quarry Books, a member of Quarto Publishing Group USA Inc.
100 Cummings Center
Suite 406-L
Beverly, Massachusetts 01915-6101
Telephone: (978) 282-9590
Fax: (978) 283-2742
www.quarrybooks.com

Visit www.QuarrySPOON.com and help us celebrate food
and culture one spoonful at a time!

10 9 8 7 6 5 4 3 2 1

ISBN: 978-1-63159-037-5

Digital edition published in 2015
eISBN: 978-1-62788-334-4

Library of Congress Cataloging-in-Publication Data is available

Design: Jonathan Hanahan & Dani LaFountaine, Milieu
Photography: Ayla Hibri

Printed in China

CONTENTS

INTRODUCTION

Do you **really** need another cookbook? How many do **you** already own? What would you use it for? Do you ever open a cookbook to cook? Or **it is** more like a perfect object to look at? Do I **sound** like your mom? If so, I'd rather evoke her, **not** by reprimanding you, but by cooking **with** you!

Why? Because no one can teach cooking. And no one can be taught to cook. You just cook! Like you breathe, you live, you make love, you walk … no one taught you how to walk. Can you imagine? "Put your right foot in front, lean on it, then move the left farther ahead … !" You have never said this or heard this being told to a one-year-old toddler. That child just tried to walk, and you just stood by, watching and encouraging, until he or she walked alone!

So, you just cook! And you cook for so many reasons: because you need to feed yourself; because you need to feed your family; because you need to gather around what can be shared by a group, a tribe of family, or friends; because you want to treat yourself and others; because you can communicate love and caring through a bite; because this is how you live; or because this is how you can perpetuate what you lived.

Sales of books in most literary genres are down—except for food and drink, and religion! Is food the new religion? Do "foodies" find in food and cooking the life they dream about and aspire to? There are many chefs, cooks, and "lifestylers" who will tell you, and issue edicts, on what must be done, eaten, and bought … for a better life!

As British journalist Steven Poole, author of *You Aren't What You Eat*, says, "We no longer trust politicians or the clergy; but we are hungry for cooks to tell us not just how to eat but how to live, the moralistic synecdoche easily accomplished since we now happily accept that one lives through eating."

The Orchards of Jeita

In Lebanon, I grew up around orchards in Jeita, a small village close to Beirut that is known for its wonderful caves. Men were busy in the gardens, planting herbs and salad greens and harvesting citrus fruits and almonds. And women were busy in the kitchens, transforming the gardens' bounties into what we ate for breakfast, lunch, and dinner—and competing over who could do what best. Obviously, each one thought all that she did was the best and looked with pity on the lesser good the others did!

My mother had her cahier de recettes, a notebook of handwritten recipes of dishes or cakes she had tasted, and so recorded recipes like kèke tante Eugénie (a cake, in her own way of writing English—when she knew French but not English!) and osmalyieh de Thérèse (a pastry), but never a main dish. And she had an old French dessert cookbook, inherited from a nun in the nearby convent, written by Henri-Paul Pellaprat, who wrote the cooking bible of every French household in the old days. Main dishes were never in the cahier de recettes. How could they be? Baking was one thing, but cooking was just understood. It was never written, never taught. You just cook!

You just join a cook in the kitchen, help and watch, and you will learn—not the recipe, but the way. And then you will make it your own way. We all learn the same alphabet, but no two people ever write the same way.

In school, I studied graphic design. But I never worked in it. I worked at Art et Culture, the first cultural center that sprouted after the civil war in Lebanon ended (1991), and that was a great teaching time in my life. I saw people from all regions, the different religions and politics of Lebanon, those who were fighting yesterday but were coming together then around art and culture. It was a common ground that could bring them all together, looking for similarities beyond their differences.

And so I started touring a country I had lived in but had never known (Lebanon during the war was divided into many unreachable parts) and started discovering wonderful people, the same everywhere, who had in common a land, an agriculture, and a cuisine.

I started writing about travel and food, about places, traditions, the hows and whys, trying to understand a bit better this patchwork that was Lebanon. It's a place like nowhere else in the world, where everyone is "the one" and "the other" at the same time, and where everybody is part of a bigger mosaic that tries to stick together as much as possible: Christians and Muslims, sea people and mountain people, those looking to the East and those looking to the West… all trying to make one together!

Then I developed an interest in macrobiotics and in the Slow Food movement. In the spring of 2004, the first

Garden Show took place in Beirut's pine forest, and I was in charge of the food section. I gathered ten of the producers and farmers I knew for a five-day event. It was very successful, and so the decision was made to go on with a weekly farmers' market, every Saturday morning in downtown Beirut. It is a producers-only market, gathering the best of our land, fields, and kitchens and the best of our farmers, producers, and cooks. Souk el Tayeb was born, and it later developed into an organization with many different activities promoting sustainable agriculture, including the farmers' market, the regional food festivals, the food training programs, and Tawlet, the farmers' kitchen. Tawlet is a social business, where profit is generated to support farmers, cooks, and food producers.

Still, this is not a book about Souk el Tayeb or about Tawlet, not about the smiling Georgina, the strict Zeina, the many-times-wedded Abou Rabih, or the grandpa Shawki: Their stories and life adventures are to be told in many other pages and places.

About This Book

In this book, I want to tell you about my country—the land, the produce, the dishes, the celebrations—not in any old way, but through a very specific cuisine: akl b' zeit. The literal translation would be "food in oil"; however, this does not mean that the food is swimming in oil, but rather that it is cooked with oil as opposed to butter, ghee, or any animal product. And understand that oil means olive oil, as nothing else existed in the old times.

Akl b' zeit is the vegetarian cuisine of Lebanon—though this is not a vegetarian book. All world cuisines have vegetarian recipes, but Lebanese cuisine has a specific vegetarian tradition. Vegetables and herbs (wild or cultivated) were abundant and so were a main base for most of the cuisine. Everything can be cooked either with meat or b' zeit, from beans to stews to spinach. Akl b' zeit is a cuisine of the land and of the seasons. Meat was scarce and precious and so was saved for Sunday's meal, and it was never eaten on its own, as a big steak or a roast, but was always instead accompanied by a grain, like rice

or bulgur: in other words, a bit of meat and a lot of grains and vegetables!

Akl b' zeit is also a necessity to comply with the religious requirements of the Christians, Catholics (Maronite, Greek Catholic, Latin, and so on) and Orthodox, where fasting is observed for the Lenten period (from midnight to noon) before Easter and for many other occasions too. And where abstinence from meat is observed, the food is referred to as akl aateh, literally "cut food," meaning food "cut" or absent from meat. The "cut" varies in different traditions. The Orthodox Lenten tradition is the strictest, with atee' el baiaad," or "cut from the whites," meaning that eggs, cheese, butter, and even honey are prohibited.

Public Cuisine and Private Cuisine

Lebanese cuisine is divided into two very distinct parts: public cuisine, which is to say street food and restaurant food; and private cuisine, or what people cook and eat at home. For a foreigner visiting Lebanon, Lebanese food is public food, specifically mezze. It's a sacred procession that starts with tabouleh and/or fattoush; followed by cold mezze (small dishes, not to say appetizers, as the meal is not built around appetizers and mains, but rather around a succession of different small dishes), such as thyme salad, hummus, moutabal (eggplant dip), and white bean salad; followed by raw meat (fillet pieces, kibbeh, or kofte); followed by hot mezze, such as fried potatoes with coriander, fried kibbeh, and pies; and ending with skewers of either barbecued meat, chicken, kofte, and so on, or grilled fish and other seafood. A mezze is either of land (meat and chicken) or of sea (fish and seafood). The chapter on Souk and Street Food gives you some classic examples of Lebanese public cuisine.

Home cuisine is very different from restaurant cuisine. A lunch at home, whether everyday or Sunday lunch, is never a mezze affair. Some dishes of the mezze table can be included, but they are served in a different combination. A home meal is built around home-style cuisine, such as stews and typical regional and traditional dishes. Most of the recipes in this book are from the tradition of private, or home, cuisine.

Home cuisine is related to the land, too, and shows two main variations: an urban cuisine, built around abundance and sophisticated ingredients and techniques, and a more rustic rural, mainly mountainous cuisine, built around wheat, bulgur, and preserves, including keshek (fermented bulgur and yogurt) and awarma (preserved meat).

Kibbeh or Kebbeh

You say to-may-to, I say to-mah-to. You will encounter many new ingredient names in this book. None of the ingredients themselves are too exotic for the home kitchen, but to help with your comfort level, I have made some spellings more familiar and "Westernized." For example, is it kibbi, kibbe, kibbeh, or kebbeh? I would definitely use the latter, as it is the closest to the original! Personally, I also prefer hommos to hummus, and burghol to bulgur, for the same reason. But this is not what we chose for this book. I also like to keep the dishes' names in their original language, in Arabic, and so you will see many instances of Arabic transliteration in these pages.

Cooking Times

In many of these recipes, I instruct you to cook something until it is done! That is, until the beans are softened, or the rice is soft but not mushy, or the bread is golden. Why should everything be timed? Can't you just taste as you go and evaluate accordingly? Not all gas or electric burners are the same, not all ovens are equally hot, different pots will cause boiling water to evaporate faster, and so on. Likewise, with ingredients, my long-grain rice and dried beans may be quite different in origin and hardness from your long-grain rice and dried beans and so will cook differently.

You just need to know, understand, and listen to your intuitions and feelings. You need to understand what a dish is, how it tastes, and how it is prepared; first understand the way, then do it your way. It becomes your own expression of a dish. Please don't be afraid to cook

this way! You are not in front of ruthless judges here; you are just doing the best you can, in your own way.

It comes back to what I said earlier: Just cook! This is how you learn.

Food as a Window

Food is the best way to look into people's lives. Food is the most sincere and authentic expression of traditions and history. There is no better way to understand mountain life than through mouneh (food preserves) preparation at the end of summer, to save the summer's bounties for the cold days of winter. There is no better way to understand the rich and sophisticated coastal cities than through halawet el jeben (sweet melting cheese rolls, scented with orange blossom and roses, wrapped around ashta, Arabic cream) or samkeh harra (cold fish in coriander and lemon). To share food and recipes is to speak best about oneself, to share a piece of oneself with another, and to express what and who we are through a pasta dish, a traditional cheese, or a rice roll.

Food should never be about who makes what best and faster. It is about telling a story, preserving a tradition, making new ones, and feeding with delicious bites and emotion those we love.

KIBBEH

If Lebanon were a dish, would it be a tabouleh, a manousheh (flatbread), or a kibbeh? Of all traditional Lebanese dishes, nothing has as many regional variations and interpretations as kibbeh.

Kibbeh is a very finely minced puréed mixture—mainly of meat or fish, or in vegetarian versions pumpkin, lentils, or potatoes—and fine bulgur, seasoned with onion, salt, pepper, and fragrant herbs. Marjoram is the kibbeh herb, and a pot of it growing on a windowsill is a must in every house.

From Zgharta's purest kibbeh to the South's most fragrant the'wishet kebbeh to the vegetarian versions or the Armenian vospov kofte (Armenian for "lentil kibbeh"), it is hard to choose. Even so, Zgharta is the kibbeh capital of Lebanon, the place where kibbeh has evolved into more than 30 different recipes, shapes, tastes, and mixtures. There is kebbeh nayieh (raw meat kibbeh, a must on a mezze table), arrass (fried kibbeh balls), sanyieh (oven baked in a pan), bi-laban (in a yogurt sauce), arnabyieh (orange and tahini sauce), batata (potato), hummus (chickpea), and many more.

The traditional way to obtain the fine, smooth meat purée was to hand-grind the meat in a jorn (a huge stone mortar), in the Northern style; or to "beat" it on a blatta (a white marble plaque) with a wooden hammer, in the Southern style. The texture of the meat ground in this way is incomparable, as it keeps some bite to it, even if finely puréed. Nowadays, when making kibbeh at home, we use a meat grinder or food processor.

pumpkin kibbeh
(kebbet laa'tin)

Yield: 4 servings

———

For the stuffing:

¼ cup (50 g) dried chickpeas

1 medium yellow onion

1 tablespoon (15 ml) olive oil

14 ounces (390 g) sorrel (or Swiss
   chard or kale), finely chopped

1 tablespoon (6 g) ground sumac

⅓ teaspoon of 7 spices
   (see page 125)

Salt

2 ¼ pounds (1 kg) pumpkin

2 cups (320 g) bulgur

2 tablespoons (16 g) all-purpose **flour**

Zest of 1 lemon

Zest of 1 orange

2 sprigs of marjoram

2 sprigs of basil

1 medium yellow onion

Salt

Vegetable oil, for frying

A Lenten staple, *kebbet laa'tin* is the definitive mountain vegetarian kibbeh. It is easy to prepare with the garden's bounty of pumpkin (which keeps all year and from harvest to harvest) and wild herbs, the best of which is obviously *homeyda*, the spring wild sorrel leaves, which add a special lemony taste to the stuffing. If they are unavailable, you could use other leafy greens, such as Swiss chard (the best option after the sorrel) or a mix of available wild leafy greens (kale does a great job in kale countries!). You could try spinach, but sometimes it can be too watery. No matter which alternative you choose, a bit more sumac will give the desired lemony taste. The kibbeh balls keep well uncooked in the freezer.

———

To prepare the stuffing, soak the chickpeas overnight in water to cover. Drain and rub in a kitchen towel to take off the outer skin. Break each chickpea in half. Peeled and halved chickpeas are nicer and tastier in the stuffing. Boil the chickpeas in water to cover for 20 minutes and then drain.

Chop the onion. Heat the olive oil in a skillet over medium heat and sauté the onion until translucent. Add the cooked chickpeas and the sorrel and stir just to mix well; lower the heat. Season with the sumac, the 7 spices, and salt to taste.

Peel the pumpkin and cut it into cubes. Boil in water to cover for 20 minutes until tender and then drain and squeeze well with your hands.

Add the bulgur (without washing or soaking it) to the warm pumpkin and knead well to soak the bulgur. Add the flour as needed to obtain a good dough. Add the lemon and orange zests. Finely chop the marjoram and basil, finely grate the onion, and add to the mixture. Season to taste with salt.

Heat a few inches of vegetable oil in a deep pot or skillet until hot. Shape the kibbeh into walnut-size balls (see page 16) and then deep-fry in the hot oil until light gold all over. Let drain and cool on paper towels. Serve at room temperature.

SHAPING KIBBEH BALLS:
A TRIBAL AFFAIR

Learning to shape kibbeh balls properly is required to obtain the title of a proper housewife. A kibbeh (kbaibet) is shaped like a rugby ball (other shapes, and names, exist, but let's stick to rugby for now!), with pointed ends, the thinnest crust of kibbeh, and the maximum amount of stuffing ... it is not very easy for a beginner! But it is possible to learn.

To shape a kibbeh ball, take a walnut-size piece of kibbeh dough, form it into a round, and, holding it with your left hand, start digging into it with your right index finger to shape a round bowl. Dip your finger into cold water so it doesn't stick to the kibbeh and turn the bowl in the palm of your left hand, with your right index finger digging into it to build a deeper bowl, more like a drinking glass shape by now, with thin walls (the elastic consistency of the kibbeh dough is crucial to success). When thin enough, put the stuffing inside and close its upper part in a pointed shape. Work the other side to make it pointed, and then seal it all with wet fingers to obtain a smooth surface.

Many (or most) kitchen chores are (or used to be!) a tribal affair. Women are not alone in the kitchen for such "impossible tasks" as rolling grape leaves, baking maa'moul, or shaping kibbeh balls. Rather, family women, or neighbors, all get together around the working table and get the "impossible tasks" done. In a group, it's faster and easier, and it has the air of a social gathering. The task maestro is often the grandma, and she is the one to distribute the jobs and to check on the end result.

KEBBET HILLEH:
THE "TRICKY KIBBEH" OF MAR TEDROS

The countryside around Byblos and Batroun is scattered with old churches, often dating to the Paleochristian era, built with some antique reused materials (Roman and Byzantine), with walls covered in medieval frescoes, in a typical local style, mixing Byzantine and occidental expressions. Behdidet is a small village with an old square church set amid almond trees, overlooking the blue sea and the ancient city of Byblos. Mar Tedros church, the church of Saint Theodorus, has beautifully preserved frescoes, which have been recently restored.

An old priest there, who looked as ancient as the church itself, loved to tell the story of the patron saint, Saint Theodoros. The saint is said to have been a Roman army general at the time of the persecutions of Christians. One day, he knew there were going to be house searches for Christians on a Friday (the day of fasting from meat), and so he secretly sent a message to the Christian community telling them to find a solution to trick the soldiers! They created a vegetarian version of kibbeh (which didn't exist before, according to the priest), and it fooled the soldiers into thinking the Christians were eating a meat kibbeh, and therefore they couldn't find or catch the Christians. Tricky kibbeh!

potato kibbeh

(kebbet batata nayeh)

Yield: 4 servings

---

2 ¼ pounds (1 kg) potatoes

1 ¼ cups (200 g) fine bulgur

1 ½ cups (150 g) walnuts

1 scallion

1 fresh green chile pepper

2 sprigs of thyme

2 sprigs of mint

Pinch of ground nutmeg

Salt

6 tablespoons (90 ml) olive oil

This is one of the easiest kibbeh to do, as no shaping dexterity is needed! *Kebbet batata*, or potato kibbeh, comes in two versions. In this version, nayeh means "raw"; not that the potato is raw, because it is boiled and cooked, but rather that it is mixed with bulgur and herbs and eaten without further cooking. In a variation, this same kibbeh is layered in a baking pan, with a stuffing of onions and walnuts in the middle, and baked to get crispy. This unbaked version is a hearty and fragrant alternative to mashed potatoes.

Boil the whole potatoes in water to cover until well cooked. Meanwhile, wash the bulgur, squeeze it well with your hands, and place in a bowl. In an electric mixer or food processor, chop the walnuts and scallion and then add the chile pepper, thyme, and mint and blend just for a moment or two (so as not to bruise the green herbs).

Peel the hot potatoes, mash with a fork or a potato masher (but not in a mixer, as it will turn gluey), and mix with the bulgur. Season with the nutmeg and salt to taste. Knead together well. Let it cool a bit before adding the nut-herb mixture (so that the herbs don't blacken). Flatten onto a serving plate and serve drizzled with the olive oil.

JNOUBIEH ...
SOUTHERN STYLE!

Kibbeh has two camps: Northern and Southern. You have to choose one camp.

Northern style is pure and simple: In the village of Ehden, a *kebbeh nayeh* is made of just meat (goat, obviously), bulgur, salt, and white pepper and nothing else. Why does it need anything if it is perfect as it is? It's the pure taste of perfect ingredients!

Southern style, on the other hand, is all you can add! Women head to the garden for a *tehwisheh*, a "picking," and they will pick and gather fragrant aromatics to add to their kibbeh: a mix of fresh marjoram, basil, *ooter* (fragrant geranium), *beatriin* (wild mint), parsley, hot chile pepper, and green bell pepper; and then also dried cumin, rosebuds, marjoram, cinnamon, and salt. All are finely ground and mixed with the bulgur, which will take on a sort of fluorescent green color.

This bulgur is added to raw meat for a *kebbeh nayeh jnoubyieh* (Southern raw kibbeh) or used in a vegetarian version, with mashed potato, for a green *kebbet batata*.

armenian lentil kibbeh

(vospov kofte)

Yield: 4 servings

────────

1 cup (192 g) split yellow lentils

1 medium yellow onion

3 tablespoons (45 ml) olive oil

3 scallions

½ bunch flat-leaf parsley

½ cup + 2 tablespoons (100 g)
   fine-grind white bulgur

1 teaspoon salt

½ teaspoon ground cumin

½ teaspoon paprika

¼ teaspoon cayenne pepper
   (optional)

For the garnish:

1 medium tomato

1 cucumber

1 scallion

1 small green bell pepper

2 or 3 sprigs flat-leaf parsley,
   plus a few leaves for more garnish

Pinch of salt

Pinch of ground cumin

Ground sumac

Here's another version of kibbeh, prepared the Armenian way. It's a kibbeh of bulgur and fragrant herbs with cooked split yellow lentils. *Vospov kofte* is a Lenten dish and a perfect option for a light and nutritious summer meal. Armenian cuisine is best known for its *soujouk* (spicy sausage), *mante* (meat-filled ravioli in a yogurt sauce), and *lahm b'ajin* (meat pies), but other Armenian home-cooked dishes such as this are definitely worth discovering.

────────────

Rinse and drain the lentils, place in a pot, add fresh water to cover, and bring to a boil. Skim off the foam when it forms at the surface and let it simmer for about 30 minutes until the lentils are very well cooked, mushy, and form a thick paste. Stir occasionally to help break the lentils into a paste.

Meanwhile, finely chop the onion. Heat the olive oil in a skillet and sauté the onion until lightly golden. Finely chop the scallions and the parsley.

Mix the cooked lentils, cooked onion, scallions, parsley, bulgur, salt, cumin, paprika, and cayenne and knead everything together to form a homogeneous mix. It must be as thick as a dough, not too runny and not too stiff. If it is too stiff, add a few drops of olive oil and water. If it is too runny, let it cool a bit, and it should get firmer.

For the garnish, finely chop the tomato, cucumber, scallion, pepper, and parsley sprigs and mix all together with the salt and cumin. Season to taste with sumac.

Shape the kibbeh into pieces the size and shape of fingers, garnish with parsley leaves, and serve along with the additional garnish.

BOURJ HAMMOUD
ARMENIATOWN

Nahr Beirut (Beirut's river) traces the northern limit of the city, and it is believed to be the place where Saint George slew the dragon. Thus Beirut's bay is called Saint George; and the city's main Maronite and Orthodox churches are dedicated to St. George; and close to the river is Al Khodr shrine and mosque, a Shiite mosque dedicated to Al Khodr, ("the Green"), a sainted person who has the same attributes as Saint George.

On the other side of the river is Bourj Hammoud, the Armenian quarter of the city. It has been this way since 1915, as founded by the survivors of the Armenian genocide who arrived to Lebanon and settled in camps in Bourj Hammoud and in Aanjar, in the Beqaa Valley. Welcome to Armenia, where the streets have Armenian names, the food is Armenian, and the people, the crafts, the houses are Armenian.

Today, Bourj Hammoud is one of the most densely populated districts in the region, with narrow streets, commerce on the street level, and houses above. Of all the streets of Bourj Hammoud, Marash is the most interesting—because it is the food street! Shops spill into the street (more of a narrow alley, one should say) with the best of the Armenian specialties: Lahm b'ajin (meat pies) is the top Armenian food specialty, along with soujouk (spicy sausages) and basterma (Armenian-style pastrami, dried meat fillet seasoned under a paste of salt, fenugreek, and other spices). There is also reb el harr (hot chile paste), paprika, walnuts, walnuts in grape molasses, cheese in threads, pomegranates, festive Armenian sweets (there is even an "engagement" sweet), and much more.

Bourj Hammoud has its restaurants, too, including Varouj, a hole in the wall for the tastiest Armenian mezze. There is also Onno, as small and as good with some more home-style staples. And the newcomer is Badeguer, in a restored old house, with traditional home cuisine only.

fish kibbeh

(kebbet samak)

Yield: 4 servings

————

4 ¾ cups (760 g) fine-grind bulgur

2 ½ pounds (1 kg) firm white fish
   fillets, such as red snapper or bass

3 pounds (1.4 kg) yellow onions

Zest of 1 lemon

Zest of 1 orange

2 bunches of green coriander

4 teaspoons (8 g) ground coriander

½ teaspoon ground allspice

½ teaspoon ground cumin

½ teaspoon salt

5 ½ tablespoons (50 g) pine nuts

½ teaspoon crushed red chile flakes

1 cup (235 ml) vegetable oil

Kibbeh is mainly done with meat, with more than 30 different versions of it, but in coastal cities, kibbeh is made with fish! This is an easy-to-do recipe, as no special shaping skills are needed. The kibbeh is just layered in a baking pan, with stuffing below and one layer of kibbeh above it. *Kebbet samak* is perfumed with the coastal fragrances of seafood and orange and lemon zest.

————————

Preheat the oven to 425°F (220°C, or gas mark 7).

Wash the bulgur and squeeze well.

Cut the fish fillets and ½ pound (225 g) of the onions into big chunks. Add the zest of the lemon and the orange, the green coriander, 2 teaspoons of the ground coriander, the allspice, cumin, and salt and pass the mixture through a meat grinder to obtain a uniform kibbeh dough (a meat grinder is a better option here than an electric mixer or a food processor, which would turn the fish mixture too mushy).

Cut the remaining 2 ¼ pounds (1 kg) of onions into thin slices. Add the pine nuts, the remaining 2 teaspoons ground coriander, the red chile flakes, and ½ cup (120 ml) of the vegetable oil. Combine well and spread in the bottom of a 12-inch (30 cm) square baking pan.

Form the kibbeh into balls and then flatten them into disks to cover the pan. When all the stuffing is covered, wet your hand with cold water and beat down the surface of the kibbeh to compact it into the pan. Smooth the surface. A kibbeh should be nice to look at as well as to taste; for that, draw patterns on the surface, using a knife that will just draw on the surface without cutting into it. Draw sun patterns in a round pan or rectangular ones in a rectangular pan. Cover the kibbeh with the remaining vegetable oil and bake for 30 minutes until it turns gold and crispy on the surface.

GRAINS

History shifted when men started planting grains and transitioned from being hunter-gatherers, always on the run after new animals to hunt, to farmers who planted seeds and needed to wait for them to grow in order to harvest them. During this wait, men started settling, building homes, and extending them into groups, communities, villages, and cities.

Each region has its grain: rice in Asia, buckwheat in Russia, quinoa in South America—and wheat in the Levant. Wheat is rarely consumed as is, but is transformed into bulgur, frikeh, and flour. Wheat berries are cooked whole for hrisseh, a mountain party food, where meat (or chicken) and the wheat berries are cooked for hours in huge caldrons until everything metamorphoses into a thick and delicious porridge. And they are cooked whole for qamhyieh, boiled wheat berries served with nuts and sugar for the Barbara, our local Halloween, or for the first tooth of a child, when it is called snaynyieh.

Bulgur is not simply cracked wheat because when raw wheat is just cracked, the cooked result is coarse and gruel-like and not bulgur. To prepare bulgur, wheat is boiled until half cooked (so the starch cooks), then sun-dried, then cracked, so the cracked grain has a uniform amber color and hard texture. Bulgur can be made from white or brown wheat, with bulgur from brown wheat being nuttier and tastier.

Frikeh is a wheat product too, made from roasted green wheat, and can be whole or cracked. Wheat stalks are picked at a certain point of maturity, when the berries are still green, and the berries are dried in a fire, which adds a specific smoked flavor to the wheat berries. The berries can then be left whole or cracked. Frikeh is a delicious and rare delicacy that deserves a lot of buzz. I hope that it may soon become the new quinoa, a darling of chefs and restaurateurs who are always on the hunt for the newest exotic discovery.

bulgur with tomatoes and peppers

(burghol aa' banadoura)

An easy summer dish to serve with *laban* (yogurt), *burghol aa' banadoura* could be thought of as our local risotto! It's very simple to prepare, needing just a few ingredients that are always on hand. Still, the secret of a good *burghol aa' banadoura* is a flavor that must be a bit spicy and a consistency that must not be too hard or too runny, but rather made up of moist and tender flakes of bulgur.

Yield: 4 servings

————

1 medium yellow onion

1 green bell pepper

1 fresh red or green chile pepper

¼ cup (60 ml) olive oil

2 ½ cups (400 g) coarse-grind white bulgur (or whole bulgur)

2 ¼ pounds (1 kg) tomatoes

2 garlic cloves, peeled

1 tablespoon (16 g) tomato paste (optional)

¼ teaspoon ground white pepper

Salt

Yogurt, for serving

Finely chop the onion, bell pepper, and chile pepper. Heat the oil in a large skillet over medium heat and sauté the vegetables for 5 minutes. Meanwhile, wash the bulgur and let it soak in the water.

Peel the tomatoes, if desired (blanch them in boiling water for a minute to loosen the skins), and blend with the garlic in a blender or food processor until puréed. Add to the onion, bring to a boil, and let it boil for 5 minutes. If the tomato sauce is not red enough, add the tomato paste.

Drain the bulgur and add it to the tomato sauce. Add the white pepper and season to taste with salt, bring to a boil, and then lower the heat and cook until the bulgur is tender and has absorbed all the liquid. Serve warm, with yogurt on the side.

bulgur with mixed vegetables

(makmoura)

Makmoura, or *mattmoura*, means "buried," referring to the vegetables buried in the bulgur. This is a very typical mountain dish ... if you say bulgur, you say mountain dish!

Yield: 4 servings

---

2 medium yellow onions

¼ cup (60 ml) olive oil

18 ounces (510 g) romano (flat) green beans

18 ounces (510 g) zucchini

2 ¼ pounds (1 kg) tomatoes

1 ¾ cups (280 g) coarse-grind white bulgur

Salt

Yogurt, for serving

Finely chop the onions. Heat the olive oil in a large skillet over medium heat and sauté the onions until translucent, about 5 to 10 minutes. Cut the green beans in half and add to the onions. Sauté for 10 minutes or until the green beans are softened. Cut the zucchini into big chunks and add to the green beans. Peel the tomatoes, if desired (blanch them in boiling water for a minute to loosen the skins), cut into chunks, and add them to the skillet. Bring to a boil, and then lower the heat and simmer gently until the vegetables are nearly cooked.

Wash and drain the bulgur and add to the vegetables. Season to taste with salt. The juices must cover the surface of the bulgur and vegetable mixture. If not, add a bit of water. Cook over a low fire until the bulgur absorbs the juices and is fully cooked. Serve warm.

Yogurt is a perfect accompaniment to all bulgur dishes.

BULGUR: THE STAPLE OF LEBANESE CUISINE

Bulgur, burghul, or burghol … I actually prefer the last spelling, as it is the closest to the original name in Arabic, though bulgur is more familiar to many English speakers. Whatever you call it, though, bulgur is common in the cuisines of Lebanon, Syria, Turkey, Armenia, and Palestine.

Though it is often referred to as "cracked wheat," this is doesn't really describe it properly. Bulgur is wheat that has been parboiled, partially cooked to transform its starch, and then sun-dried, and only then cracked into different thicknesses.

Fine-ground bulgur is used for tabouleh and kibbeh. It does not need cooking and can be just added raw to a tabouleh (for those who like it cracking!), or just rinsed in water, or added to the chopped tomato to soak in their juices (my favorite version).

Coarse-ground bulgur is larger and so needs cooking. It is used instead of rice to accompany a stew (like rez mfalfal) or for stuffing vegetables. Eggplants are perfect stuffed with bulgur and meat and cooked in a sumac sauce. Coarse bulgur is cooked like a risotto as well, with tomato, vegetables, or meat (burghol bi dfinn).

Burghol kaser (broken) describes when the grain is just cracked in half, "broken" into two pieces, which makes it the coarsest version, and easy to cook.

Sraysira is the finest grind, a flour-like type of bulgur that is used to thicken kibbeh or make some kinds of bread, like the Southern jrish.

Bulgur, in all its shapes and sizes, is the main cereal of mouneh (food preserves). And it is the main ingredient of keshek, which is fermented yogurt and bulgur that is sun-dried, then transformed in a powder that will keep for a whole year, and will be cooked as a soup, stew, or filling for pies (fatayer).

bulgur with cabbage and chile

(marshousheh)

Yield: 4 servings

————

½ cup + 2 tablespoons (100 g)
   coarse-grind brown bulgur
2 medium yellow onions
¼ cup (60 ml) olive oil
2 ¼ pounds (1 kg) white cabbage
1 fresh red or green chile pepper
Salt

Marshousheh means "the scattered" and is simply scattered bulgur over cooked cabbage. Easy! This recipe represents the epitome of mountain food: simple, rustic, filling, and easy to prepare. The simple ingredients include onion (obviously every-where!), cabbage (the perfect winter vegetable), a handful of coarse bulgur, and just a pinch of salt.

————

Wash the bulgur and let it soak in just enough water to cover the surface until the bulgur has soaked up the water, about 10 minutes or so.

Finely chop the onions. Heat the olive oil in a large skillet over medium heat and sauté the onions until translucent. Meanwhile, chop the cabbage and chile pepper and add to the onions.

Add the bulgur, season to taste with salt, and stir to mix all the ingredients.

Lower the heat and cook until the cabbage and bulgur are cooked to your taste, stirring often so that it doesn't stick. Serve warm.

smoked green wheat with vegetables

(frikeh bel khodra)

Frikeh is a specialty of South Lebanon, Palestine, and Southern regions of Syria. Zeinab Kashmar has devised the best way to cook frikeh: She sautés the grains to add to their nutty, smoky taste. Her frikeh is so tasty that it needs no accompaniment of meat of chicken, but is perfect on its own, with just grilled vegetables.

Whole frikeh is nice looking but doesn't melt well into the sauce. Cracked frikeh cooks up more risotto-like. The best option here, if possible, is to have a mix of half and half!

Yield: 4 servings

————

3 medium yellow onions

¼ cup (60 ml) vegetable oil

1 cup (184 g) frikeh
   (roasted green wheat)

6 scallions

2 zucchini

2 carrots

2 tablespoons (28 ml) olive oil

½ teaspoon ground black pepper

Salt

Finely chop the onions. Heat the vegetable oil in a large skillet over medium-low heat and sauté the onions until they break down and caramelize, about 20 to 30 minutes. Stir often so that the onions color evenly and don't burn or stick. The onion pieces should melt by the end and not show in the frikeh.

Wash and drain the frikeh. Do not let the frikeh steep in the water, as it will lose it smoky taste. Add the frikeh to the caramelized onions and continue stirring and frying to add the smoky flavor of the frikeh to the mixture. When the mixture is dry enough, it will start to stick, so you will know that it is done.

At this stage, frikeh can be stored in the fridge to finish cooking later. Or add enough water to cover the grains by a finger and let them cook over low heat until all the water is absorbed.

Meanwhile, prepare the grilled vegetables. Preheat a stovetop grill pan or an outdoor grill. Trim the scallions and cut the carrots and zucchini into slices. Drizzle with the olive oil and season with the black pepper and salt to taste. Grill until softened with good grill marks (put the carrots on first, as they will obviously take longer than the scallions and zucchini to soften).

Serve the frikeh hot with the grilled vegetables.

armenian fine bulgur salad

(itch)

Yield: 4 servings

————

2 medium yellow onions

1 cup (120 ml) vegetable oil

2 ¼ pounds (1 kg) tomatoes

1 green bell pepper

1 cup (160 g) fine-grind white bulgur

Juice of 3 lemons

1 tablespoon (16 g) red chile paste

1 tablespoon (20 g) debs el remmen
    (pomegranate molasses)

Salt

When the Armenians arrived in Lebanon in the early twentieth century, they settled in Bourj Hammoud and in Aanjar and brought with them their traditions, skills, and cuisine. Armenian cuisine is sophisticated and has a taste of its own. *Itch* is basically the Armenian version of a tabouleh. Itch is mainly fine-ground bulgur soaked in a tomato-based sauce. Sona Tikidjian is the queen of Armenian cuisine at Tawlet and the sweetest cook and person you will ever meet! Her *itch* is perfect in both flavor and consistency—not too thick and not too soupy!

Finely chop the onions. Heat the vegetable oil in a large skillet over medium heat and sauté the onions until translucent. Peel and dice the tomatoes. Finely chop the green pepper and add the green pepper and tomatoes to the onions. Bring to a boil and then lower the heat and cook for 15 minutes until the tomatoes start melting.

Take the skillet off the heat and add the bulgur, lemon juice, chile paste, and pomegranate molasses. Season to taste with salt. Mix well and let the bulgur soak up all the juices. Serve at room temperature.

FRIKEH STORIES

Frikeh comes from the verb faraka, "to rub"— so frikeh means "rubbed," as the grains are rubbed by hand, after being dried in the fire, to take off the outer bran.

Frikeh is simply wheat harvested in its last "green" stage, before the stalks dry and turn gold. By then, the grains are fully formed but are still moist and chewy. If picked and stored this way, they will rot, so they need to be dried; they are thrown in the fire, which will dry them, preserve their green color, and add a smoked flavor to the grain.

Why go through all this fuss? Village stories say that the farmers needed to pick their wheat early, before harvest time, when taxes were higher and often soldiers would come to confiscate the harvest. Also, during World War I, Lebanon had a major famine, and all wheat and flour were confiscated by the occupying Ottoman soldiers. A special cable to *The New York Times* on September 16, 1916, reported that the "whole Levant is starving and hopeless, American woman writer says."

Frikeh production demands skill and experience. The producer must know when to pick the grain—not too soft, not too dry—and how much to roast it. Too little will not smoke it, and too much will burn it. There are also the questions of which wood to use in the smoking and how long to dry the smoked grain. There are a lot of details, which makes frikeh production a master's job.

MUJADARA

Mujadara is another regional indicator: Tell me what is in your mujadara, and I will tell you who you are! One thinks that mujadara comes in one version, the one that Mom always made. But with a wider look comes a mujadara extravaganza of many colors and versions, north to south, illustrating perfectly the regional differences, from the Northern Lebanese passionately hard feel to the Southern Lebanese soft and smooth feel. In the north, harsh mountains and hard characters bring forth a dark mujadara with caramelized onions, red beans, and bulgur. In the south, there is the soft, pale yellow, light mjadra safra (yellow mujadara), with split lentils and a bit of rice. In between (in terms of both geography and preparation!), it is "regular," made with bulgur in rice, both in a "grainy" version and a puréed version.

Mujadara is Friday's staple dish and a main dish of the Lenten period. It is always served in a shallow serving dish; poured when hot, it sets in the dish and is served at room temperature. Mujadara consistency runs from panna cotta–hard to wobbly thick yogurt. The lighter the color, the thinner the consistency! When served in its dish, we say "we break the plate," which means we break the "set" mujadara when we take some of it, and it can not be served again. It's always better to serve it in dishes only as big as needed for the correct number of people, as leftovers from the "broken plate" are not very appealing.

southern-style split lentils with rice

(mujadara safra)

This is *the* mujadara of South Lebanon. With a light yellow color and a runnier consistency, the *mujadara safra* is a perfect summer dish that is best served with radishes and olives. It's very easy to prepare, with a minimum of ingredients and preparation, and not a single kitchen machine in use! The secret of a good *mujadara safra* is in its consistency: not too runny and not too firm, but rather a yogurt-like consistency. Jiggly is good! Seasoning is intentionally kept to a minimum, so as to preserve the flavor of the ingredients, mainly the lentils.

Yield: 6 servings

———————

2 ¼ pounds (1 kg) split yellow lentils

2 cups (384 g) short-grain rice

2 medium yellow onions

2 tablespoons (28 ml) olive oil

Salt

Put the lentils in a pot with enough water to cover them by 2 fingers and bring to a boil. Lower the heat and cook until softened. Meanwhile, soak the rice in cold water. When the lentils are well cooked so that you can mash them, drain the rice and add it to the lentils. Continue cooking over low heat and add more water, if needed, to keep the water level 2 fingers above the surface of the mixture.

Meanwhile, chop the onions into small pieces. Heat the olive oil in a medium skillet over medium heat and sauté the onions till they are blond, stirring often so that they color evenly, about 20 minutes.

When the rice is cooked, add the fried onions to the pot and let cook for 10 more minutes. Season to taste with salt. The consistency must be a bit runny; add water, if needed, or if too liquidy, boil over high heat to reduce the water and thicken the mujadara.

Transfer to a shallow dish and let it set and cool before serving.

lentils and rice

(mujadara)

Yield: 4 servings

---

2 cups + 2 tablespoons (408 g)
   brown lentils

6 medium yellow onions

¼ cup (60 ml) olive oil

½ cup (96 g) short-grain rice

Salt

Ground cumin (optional)

½ cup (120 ml) vegetable oil

Mujadara is one of those dishes that incites conflictual discussions. Do you like your tabouleh's bulgur soft or crunchy? Do you prefer the red side or white side of the *khobz*, Arabic bread (pita)? Do you prefer *mouloukhyieh* (Jew's mallow) in leaves or finely chopped? They are all issues that can start a war in Lebanon—or at least some very heated and passionate discussions! For mujadara, do you prefer it as *msafayieh* ("sieved," meaning puréed) or as *moudardara* ("grainy," kept in distinct grains)?

One thing is sure: Mujadara lentils must be small, round, and dark brown. Those have a deep nutty flavor that will make all the difference for this purist's dish. In this puréed version, the texture is smooth and silky, and it goes perfectly with a cabbage salad (very thinly sliced) seasoned with a lot of lemon and dried mint and some deep red tomatoes.

Put the lentils in a pot with enough water to cover and bring to a boil.

Meanwhile, finely chop 2 of the onions and thinly slice the remaining 4 onions. Heat the olive oil in a large skillet over medium heat and sauté the chopped onions until translucent, about 10 minutes. Then add the sautéed onions, along with the rice, to the lentils when the lentils are half cooked (when you can bite through them but they are still firm). Add enough water to cover by 2 fingers.

Bring to a boil and cook until the lentils are fully cooked and tender. Season to taste with salt (some will also season a mujadara with cumin).

Purée the mixture in a blender or through a food mill. Transfer the mujadara to a plate and let it cool and set on the plate. The right consistency is very important—it should not be liquidy or rock solid. A good mujadara has the consistency of a thick jam or mashed potatoes.

Meanwhile, heat the vegetable oil in a deep skillet over medium heat and sauté the sliced onions, stirring, until the onions are a deep golden color, about 20 minutes. Drain on paper towels and let them cool. The onions should be golden and crisp. Decorate the mujadara with the fried onions and serve at room temperature.

red beans and bulgur

(mjadaret loubyieh)

Yield: 4 servings

---

1 cup (188 g) dried pink
    kidney beans

2 medium yellow onions

½ cup (120 ml) vegetable oil

3 tablespoons (26 g)
    coarse-grind bulgur

Salt

If the south has a lighter, sweeter version in *mujadra safra*, the north has it at the opposite end of the spectrum, dark and thick! The Northern Lebanese version of mujadara is made with red beans instead of lentils and coarse bulgur instead of rice. And the secret is in the caramelized onions, which will caramelize for more than an hour and will give a special taste and the color to this dish. The other secret to Northern Lebanese mujadara is the *loubiyieh jordieh*, a special kind of red bean planted at high altitude, of a pale brown color, that will turn to deep red when boiled. Pink kidney beans are a good substitute. This is simple cooking with barely more than three ingredients!

Wash and drain the pink beans and put in a pot with enough water to cover. Bring to a boil. When it starts boiling, add 1 cup (235 ml) cold water; it is said that this "shock" of cold water will help the beans cook faster.

Meanwhile, very finely chop the onions. Heat the vegetable oil in a deep skillet over medium-low heat and sauté the onions in the oil. The onions must be stirred constantly after they start to color to make sure they caramelize evenly. Caramelizing the onions takes time and patience, up to an hour, and the end result must be a thick onion paste of a deep caramel color.

Take the onions out of the oil, leaving the excess oil behind, and add them to the beans when nearly cooked. If the chopped onions did not melt into a paste, run them through a blender. Add the bulgur and season to taste with salt. Add water, if needed—it must cover the mixture in the pot by 2 fingers. Cook until the bulgur is cooked and the mixture is still a bit liquidy; the end result must be a bit runny, as it will set as it cools. Serve hot or at room temperature.

FRIDAY'S MEAL

Fridays are always odd days, don't you think? It's not the weekend yet, but everyone is in the mood of it! And this is more so in a country of different religions, where Friday is the Muslims' prayer day, and all civil servants are dismissed at 11 a.m., so as to be able to join the Friday prayers. Muslim or not, everybody enjoys this less-than-half day!

Friday is aa'zil day, too, housecleaning day, where Mom is busy around the house and squeezes lunch prep time to the shortest and the easiest. Friday's traditional lunch staples are mujadara and fattoush. Mujadara is prepared in the morning and left outside to cool and set; and fattoush is considered the "easy salad," as it does not need elaborate preparation and fine cutting like a tabouleh and can be prepared with nearly any vegetables and herbs that are on hand at home.

Fridays are Lenten days too for some Christians, who refrain from consuming meat on Fridays all year long, in remembrance of Good Friday.

grainy-style rice with lentils

(mudardara)

This is the "other" mujadara, the one that must be "grainy," with the rice in distinct separate grains and not puréed like the Lentils and Rice on page 40.

Yield: 4 servings

2 ¼ pounds (1 kg) large green lentils
3 ¼ pounds (1.5 kg) yellow onions
Vegetable oil, as needed
Salt
½ cup (93 g) long-grain rice, rinsed
1 teaspoon ground allspice

Place the lentils in a pot with enough water to cover and bring to a boil. Lower the heat and simmer while you continue.

Finely chop half of the onions and thinly slice the rest. Heat 2 tablespoons (28 ml) vegetable oil in a large skillet and sauté the chopped onions until caramelized, about 30 minutes. Add ½ teaspoon to the lentils when half cooked (you can bite through them but they are still firm), along with the rice. Season with the allspice and salt to taste. Add water, if needed, to cover the surface by 1 finger.

Lower the heat and simmer until the rice is cooked and has absorbed the water. Do not stir much during cooking, as the secret of this mujadara is to have it be "grainy," and stirring will mush it up.

Heat about 1 inch (2.5 cm) of vegetable oil in a deep skillet over medium heat and fry the onion slices until dark brown, about 20 minutes.

Drain on paper towels.

Serve the mujadara at room temperature on a plate and decorate with the fried onion slices.

lentils and rice with beef

(mujadara b' lahmeh)

Mujadara is all about being a vegetarian dish, and so a version with meat seems so contradictory and weird! But it does exist, and it is Georgina al Bayeh, Tawlet's super smiling cook from Kfar Dlekos, who initiated us to the wonders of *mujadara b' lahmeh*!

Yield: 4 servings

2 medium yellow onions

5 tablespoons (75 ml) olive oil

18 ounces (510 g) coarsely ground beef

2 ½ cups (480 g) small brown lentils, rinsed and drained

2 cups (376 g) long-grain converted rice

Salt

Finely chop the onions. Heat the olive oil in a large skillet over medium heat and sauté the onions until translucent, about 10 minutes. Add the meat and stir to crumble the meat and let it start to dry a bit. Add the lentils to the skillet. Add enough water to cover by 3 fingers and cook until the lentils are tender.

When the lentils are cooked, add the rice and a bit more water, if needed, to cover the surface by 1 finger. Season to taste with salt and cook to let the rice absorb the water. Serve warm.

STEWS

Tabakh means "to cook"—tabikh, the word for "stews," is "cooked"—and there is nothing better cooked than a stew! Stews represent everyday Lebanese cuisine and make up the basics of daily food: A meal is built around a tabkha (the singular), typically served with rice or bulgur and a salad.

Tabikh are often rather soupy and so for this reason are eaten along with a grain. Rice can be plain or with vermicelli added (maa' shh'ayryieh). Long-grain rice is perfect alongside stews, as it will not be sticky. American parboiled rice is some cooks' favorite because it is very easy to cook and never sticks, but it lacks in taste and texture. Bulgur is the original cereal of the Levant and so is a more rustic accompaniment to a meal.

Every stew is built around an alyieh, which is similar to the Italian soffritto. Alyieh is basically a sauté of minced onion that is the base of the stew, with the addition of tomato, garlic, and either coriander or mint.

GRAINY RICE
WITH VERMICELLI
(REZ MAFALFAL / MAA' SHH'AYRYIEH)

We have a saying for when someone is receiving preferential treatment: El ezz lal rozz wel burghol shanak helo ("glory to rice, and the bulgur hang itself"). Its origin goes back to the fact that bulgur is a local ingredient that has always existed in Lebanese food, and rice is an imported product that seemed to be fancier and more desirable than bulgur.

With any rice for serving with stews, the trick is to cook the rice properly, but still have each grain separate and not end up with a sticky mound of rice. Rice is first washed well in water. Grains should be rubbed and massaged and the water changed often, two or three times, until it gets nearly clear. The simplest way to cook rice is to add 1 ½ cups (355 ml) of water to every 1 cup (195 g) of rice, put it on to boil, add a pinch of salt when it starts boiling, lower the heat to a minimum, and let it absorb its water and cook. While cooking, rice should never be stirred, or it will form lumps and stick.

To figure out whether all the water has been absorbed, insert a wooden spoon or a chopstick to touch the bottom of the pan. It should feel dry and the rice should have started forming a thin crust (but not a burnt bottom). Remove from the heat at that point and keep the pot covered for at least 15 minutes. Good cooks always prepare their rice an hour before mealtime; when cooked, they take out the "rice cover" (a piece of thick old woolen blanket) and tuck it over the rice well for it to ynabett, or sprout! The rice has to cook first, and then it will "sprout" into fluffiness.

For a more flavorful version of grainy rice, rice is drained very well after being washed and then sautéed in 2 tablespoons (28 ml) of vegetable oil per 1 cup (195 g) of rice until the grains are translucent. Rez maa' shh'ayryieh is the best form of rice: 2 tablespoons (13 g) of fine, small vermicelli pieces are sautéed in 2 tablespoons (28 ml) vegetable oil until dark brown (but not black) and then the washed 1 cup (195 g) of rice is added and stirred for a minute before adding the correct amount of water and cooking as usual. The caramelized brown bits of vermicelli will contrast with the white rice and add a delicious nutty flavor and aroma to the rice.

okra stew

(yakhnet bemyieh)

Yield: 4 servings

---

3 medium yellow onions

¼ cup (60 ml) vegetable oil

1 head of garlic, cloves separated

4 medium tomatoes

1 bunch of green coriander,
   leaves and stems separated

Salt

Crushed red chile flakes

1 ¾ pounds (795 g) okra pods

1 tablespoon (20 g) debs el remmen
   (pomegranate molasses)

Bemyieh, or okra, is a fine delicacy of Lebanese cuisine. The plant itself is a beautiful shrub with pretty blue flowers that will turn into edible pods holding the plant's seeds. The trick is to choose small enough okra for them not to be tough and full of hard seeds. And the other major trick is to know how to take off each okra stem before cooking: If too short, the okra pod will be bare and give the stew an unpleasant gooey consistency. Both okra and *mouloukhyieh* (Jew's mallow) tend to transform their stew or cooking sauce into something gooey—which is something universally disliked!

Use a short, sharp knife and take off the okra stem in a circular, conical way, keeping the pod closed from its top. Frozen okra comes ready to use and makes it all that much easier!

Finely chop the onions. Heat the vegetable oil in a large skillet over low heat and sauté the onions until softened but not taking on any color, about 10 minutes. Thinly slice the garlic, add to the onion, cover the pot, and let the onion and garlic cook together over low heat until the onions are nearly melting, about 30 minutes. Peel the tomatoes, if desired (blanch them in boiling water for a minute to loosen the skins), coarsely chop them, and add to the onions.

Finely chop the coriander stems and add to the onions. Season to taste with salt and red chile flakes. The sauce should be of a nice consistency and all the vegetables nearly melted.

Add the okra and stir lightly so as not to break the fragile pods. Cook for 20 to 30 minutes.

Finely chop the coriander leaves and add to the pot, along with the pomegranate molasses. Serve hot or at room temperature.

Note:
For the bi lahmeh (meaty version), start by sautéing 14 ounces (390 g) of cubed lean beef in 2 tablespoons (28 ml) of vegetable oil and then continue with the onion as directed above. This version is served with white rice or Grainy Rice with Vermicelli (page 49).

red bean stew

(fassolia b'zeit)

Yield: 4 servings

---

1 ¼ cups (235 g) dried red
    kidney beans

4 medium tomatoes

1 head of garlic, cloves separated

1 tablespoon (16 g) tomato paste

4 medium yellow onions

½ cup (120 ml) olive oil

Salt and ground black pepper

This stew is a Lebanese home cuisine staple. Red beans are an important part of *mouneh* (food preserves) and easy to stock and cook (pink or pinto varieties are the best for this dish). The stewed beans should be soft and melting, so start with an overnight soaking (which excludes this dish from a last-minute decision!) and put them to boil (in fresh water) over low heat. The Tuscans are called "bean eaters" with good reason, and their trick for perfect bean cooking is to cook them overnight over a very low fire—ideally and traditionally, the dying embers of a wood fire.

Red Bean Stew is a Friday favorite; it can be prepared in advance and served at room temperature. It is best eaten with scallions, radishes, and a green salad.

Soak the red beans overnight in water to cover. The next day, drain, place in a large pot, cover with fresh water, bring to a boil, and let them cook over low heat until half cooked (taste the beans; if you can bite through them but they are still very firm, they are half cooked).

Meanwhile, peel the tomatoes, if desired (blanch them in boiling water for a minute to loosen the skins). Peel the garlic cloves; add the tomatoes and garlic to the half-cooked beans, along with the tomato paste. Finely chop the onions. Heat half of the olive oil in a large skillet over medium heat and sauté the onions until melting and lightly colored, about 10 to 15 minutes. Add to the beans.

Season with salt and pepper to taste and let the stew cook until the sauce is brown and thick and the beans are well cooked. How long this takes will depend on the variety and age of bean you use, so keep tasting until they are as soft as you like and the sauce is thick. When done, add the remaining olive oil and serve warm.

Note:
For the fassolia bi lahmeh (the meaty version), an oxtail is the piece of choice; its high gelatin content adds a wonderful consistency to the sauce. Start by cutting 1 ¾ pounds (795 g) oxtail into pieces and sautéing the oxtail in 2 tablespoons (28 ml) of vegetable oil until browned. Then add the soaked red beans and continue as directed above. This version is served hot, with white rice.

white butter bean stew

(yakhnet fassolia baida arrida)

Yield: 4 servings

———

3 medium yellow onions

4 garlic cloves

¼ cup (60 ml) olive oil

3 medium tomatoes

2 cups (352 g) dried white
butter beans

1 bunch of green coriander

Salt and ground black pepper

Cooked white rice, for serving

Fassolia baida arrida—big, flat, white butter beans—are considered the fanciest beans. Every good garden must have at least one plant, which will grow fast and big, like a vine, and produce large, flat, tender green pods that hold the flat white jewel-like beans. When fresh, the beans need a minimum of cooking, on very low heat, to become a melting delicacy (often seasoned with garlic, lemon, and olive oil and served as part of a mezze table). When they are in dried form, they do not need soaking overnight, as the dried bean is flat, fragile, and easy to cook.

———

Finely chop the onions and the garlic. Heat the oil in a large skillet over medium heat and sauté the onion and garlic until lightly colored, about 10 minutes.

Peel the tomatoes, if desired (blanch them in boiling water for a minute to loosen the skins), chop them, and add to the onions. Add the butter beans and enough water to cover them by a finger. Bring to a boil and then lower the heat and cook until the beans are as soft as you prefer them to be. (How long this takes will depend on the age and specific variety of bean that you use, so keep tasting!)

Finely chop the coriander and add to the cooked beans. Season to taste with salt and pepper. Serve hot, with white rice.

green fava bean stew

(foul akhdar b' zeit)

Yield: 4 servings

———

3 ¼ pounds (1.5 kg) fresh fava beans
    (in pods) or 2 ¼ pounds (1 kg)
    frozen shelled green fava beans
2 medium yellow onions
¼ cup (60 ml) olive oil
2 garlic cloves
1 bunch of green coriander
Salt

Fava beans are a staple of Lebanese cuisine. Dry green fava beans are picked in the early spring, boiled, and served as a stew-type salad for breakfast, announcing the arrival of good days and fresh eating. Big pods are laid on the side of the road for people to buy bagfuls of them and eat as nibbles along with a mezze or a beer. *Foul akhdar*, green fava, is cooked as a stew, either vegetarian or with meat. Fava pods are chosen younger, when they are fresh and tender, so as to be cooked whole, and they have a very special aroma and flavor.

If fresh fava pods are not available, you can do as well with frozen fava beans, which are generally readily available.

———

Prepare the fava pods by taking off the string at the side of the pod. Cut the pods into thumb-size pieces. If using frozen favas, thaw them.

Finely chop the onions. Heat the olive oil in a large skillet over medium heat and sauté the onions until they start to color, about 10 minutes. Finely chop the garlic and add it to the skillet. Add the fava pods. Cover and cook over very low heat for about 1 hour, so the fava pods can cook and soften without any addition of water (though you can add a bit of water, if needed).

Chop the coriander and add to the skillet. Stir well and season to taste with salt. Serve hot or at room temperature.

lemony lentil stew

(aadass bi hammod)

A definite winter warmer, *aadass bi hammod* is a thick soup/stew of lentils, Swiss chard, potatoes, onions, and lemon juice. It is a winter mountain meal, made when chard is abundant and beautiful.

Yield: 4 servings

————

1 ¼ pounds (570 g) Swiss chard

2 medium yellow onions

3 tablespoons (45 ml) olive oil

4 garlic cloves

1 medium potato

1 bunch of green coriander,
    stalks and leaves separated

1 tablespoon (6 g) ground coriander

½ cup (96 g) brown lentils

Salt

Juice of 2 lemons

Prepare the chard by separating the thick white stalks from the leaves. Finely chop the stalks and coarsely chop the leaves.

Finely chop the onions. Heat the olive oil in a large skillet over medium heat and sauté the onions until they start to color, about 10 minutes. Chop the garlic and add to the onions, along with the white chard stalks. Peel the potato, dice into cubes, and add to the skillet. Chop the coriander stalks and add to the skillet, along with the ground coriander. Add the lentils. Stir and cook all these ingredients until the mixture dries a bit and then add enough water to cover the surface by 2 fingers. Bring to a boil and then lower the heat and cook until the lentils and potato are cooked, about 40 minutes.

Add the chopped chard leaves and season to taste with salt. Cook for 10 minutes. Chop the coriander leaves and add to the pan and finish with the lemon juice. Serve hot. The consistency of this dish must not be runny like a soup, nor thick, but rather in the middle.

stewed green beans

(loubyieh b'zeit)

Yield: 4 servings

———————

2 ¼ pounds (1 kg) romano (flat)
   green beans
3 medium yellow onions
¼ cup (60 ml) olive oil
2 heads of garlic, cloves separated
1 ½ teaspoons crushed black pepper
Salt

Loubyieh b'zeit is often cooked in a tomato-based stew. I prefer by far the non-tomato version, which is loaded with garlic (cooked garlic adds sweetness to the dish) and concentrates the taste of the green beans.

String beans are unknown to traditional Lebanese gardens and cuisine. The green beans used here are flat runner beans, also known as Italian romano beans; they are not round like string beans, and they are in fact the pods of white or red beans. When left to mature, beans will develop in the pods, and when left to dry on the plant, they will become red or white beans. The best green bean variety is called *bedryieh*, as the pods do not have strings and turn meltingly soft when cooked.

Trim the green beans of any side strings and cut in half.

Finely chop the onions. Heat the oil in a large skillet over medium heat and sauté the onions until light gold, about 10 minutes. Peel the garlic cloves, but keep the cloves whole, and add to the onions. Add the green beans and black pepper and season to taste with salt. Bring to a boil and then lower the heat and cook until the beans are soft and tender. (This may take anywhere from 15 to 30 minutes, depending on the beans and your preference, so taste to be sure.) Cooking the green beans without any additional water will concentrate their flavor, but the heat must be very low for the beans to cook without drying out or burning.

Serve hot or at room temperature.

spinach stew with pine nuts

(yakhnet sbenegh)

Spinach has always had the Popeye "miracle" reputation: very nutritious, as mothers around the world have always repeated to their children! This simple stew gains so much flavor from the garlic and coriander combination, a staple of Lebanese cuisine.

Yield: 4 servings

---

4 medium yellow onions

¼ cup (60 ml) olive oil

3 ¼ pounds (1.5 kg) spinach

1 ¼ cups (170 g) pine nuts

1 tablespoon (15 ml) vegetable oil

4 garlic cloves

Salt

1 bunch of green coriander

Cooked white rice, for serving

Finely chop the onions. Heat the olive oil in a large skillet over medium heat and sauté the onions until translucent, about 5 to 10 minutes. Coarsely chop the spinach and add to the onions. The spinach melts very fast and may not need additional water to cook (the water clinging to the leaves after washing should be enough). When the mixture starts boiling, lower the heat and cook so that the spinach itself will break down and form the base of the stew.

In a small skillet over low heat, sauté the pine nuts in the vegetable oil until golden.

Crush the garlic cloves with ½ teaspoon of salt. Chop the coriander, add to the garlic, and pound a little more to obtain a coarse paste. Add the mixture to the spinach, stir well, correct the seasoning, and cook until it reaches your desired consistency.

Add the pine nuts just before serving. Serve hot, with white rice.

VEGETABLES

Vegetables are often cooked in traditional Lebanese cuisine as dishes to stand on their own, often incorporating forgotten (that is, unfashionable) vegetables, like taro root or Swiss chard. Dark leafy greens are also often served as part of a salad, but they are rarely cooked by themselves (other than boringly boiled as a side for the meat!).

Vegetables are a seasonal indicator for people as well as for nature. Fall and winter vegetables, such as cabbages, beets, and taro, are often more "rooty" and need longer cooking. Nothing proclaims spring better in Lebanon than fresh, green, crisp, lemony grape leaves. Summer produce goes even leafier and lighter. And nothing says summer better than juicy red tomatoes!

Stuffed vegetables are an important component of Lebanese cooking. Mahashi, the plural of mehsheh, translates to "stuffed" —as in stuffed vegetables. As with nearly everything, mahashi come in two versions: atee, vegetarian, and bi lahmeh, with meat.

The first is a variation on tabouleh, with parsley, tomato, onion, mint, rice (instead of bulgur), and sometimes split chickpeas, to stuff grape leaves (the best!); or it can be used to stuff small zucchini, eggplants, potatoes, green peppers, chard leaves, cabbage leaves, and in the Iraqi cuisine, onions! Vegetarian stuffed vegetables are often served as part of a mezze table or as an appetizer for a meal, rather than a main course.

Meat-stuffed vegetables, typically with a filling of short-grain rice and ground meat, are a staple of home cooking. Another version of meat stuffing features the meat only (mixed with pine nuts), which is used for koussa ablama (zucchini) or sheikh el mehsheh (eggplants—"the sheikh of the stuffed"!).

When stuffing whole vegetables or grape leaves with vegetarian filling, to prevent them from bursting, vegetables or leaves should be filled three-quarters full, as most of the stuffing ingredients are herbs and vegetables that will shrink during cooking; only the rice will expand. When stuffing whole vegetables or leaves with a meat-rice mixture, they should be filled only half full, as the meat will not lose much volume and the rice will expand.

vegetarian stuffed grape leaves

(warra' arrish atee')

Yield: 4 servings

———

5 medium tomatoes

1 small yellow onion

Salt and ground black pepper

½ cup (96 g) short-grain rice

2 bunches of flat-leaf parsley, finely chopped

1 bunch of mint, finely chopped

2 scallions, finely chopped

Ground red chile powder

Juice of 4 lemons

¼ cup (60 ml) olive oil

1 jar of grape leaves (about 60 leaves)

Grape leaves are by far the best *mehsheh* ever, in all forms and colors! Every mountain house must have a vine growing on a steel structure, over the roof (which protects from the summer sun too, and is bare in the winter, so the sun heats the roof and the house) or in its garden (perfect to sit under), for *ennab el meeydeh*, table grapes. They can be black or green, often of large size, and include varieties like *maghdousheh* (small green grapes), *vaitamouneh* (big green grapes), or *eenab kroum* (low-hanging vine grapes), and *obeidi* and *merwayih* (small grapes with a high sugar content, used for arak production). Arak is a traditional distilled alcoholic beverage in Lebanon that is made from grapes and flavored with aniseed and is somewhat similar to ouzo.

Meeydeh or *kroum*, early spring's tender grapevine leaves, are a delicacy and are eaten raw with a tabouleh or stuffed and cooked, as here. Only tender leaves are picked, as they toughen very quickly and become inedible, which makes the season very short. Because of the season's short duration, it is necessary to pick the maximum amount of tender leaves and then preserve them for the whole year by pickling, packing them tightly in a sealed jar, or nowadays more often by freezing them.

Dice 3 of the tomatoes and the onion and rub the onion with a pinch of salt and pepper. Rinse and drain the rice.

In a bowl, mix the rice, diced tomatoes and onion, parsley, mint, scallions, chile powder to taste, lemon juice, and olive oil. Season to taste with salt. Drain any excess juice from the stuffing, reserving the juice.

Start by stuffing the leaves as described on page 66. Cut the remaining 2 tomatoes into thick slices and arrange in one layer in the bottom of a large pot, to give extra moisture and flavor and to prevent the leaves on the bottom from burning or sticking to the pot. Arrange the stuffed grape leaves on top of the tomato slices in a circular pattern and close enough together so that when cooked they will form a "cake" that can be turned upside down out of the pot.

When the pot is full and well packed, add all the reserved stuffing juices to it—the liquid should just cover the leaves, so add some water if necessary. Taste the cooking liquid; it must be strongly flavored with salt, lemon, and red chile, as those will dilute during cooking and enhance the taste of the stuffed grape leaves.

Cook over low heat till the leaves are tender and the stuffing is cooked through. Let cool in the pot to allow the leaves to stick together. Then you will be able to turn the pot upside down, transfer the "cake" to a large plate, and serve it this way.

Note:
In the meat version of warra' arrish, grape leaves are stuffed full, rolled into small bundles, and arranged in layers in a pot, with lamb cutlets in the bottom of the pot and loads of garlic cloves all around. A good warra' arrish will cook for several hours on a small fire until its sauce is thick and dark green and the cutlets are meltingly soft.

WORKING WITH GRAPE
(AND OTHER) LEAVES

Filling and rolling fresh leaves can be a bit tricky to learn, but practice leads to success (and the results will always taste good, anyway!). The secret to successfully making stuffed grape leaves is to choose tender fresh leaves (hard ones will crack), as big as the palm of a (medium) hand. If all you can get are jarred leaves, they will already be softened; but they are delicate too.

Start with the non-shiny side facing you, with the tip of the leaf farthest from you. Put a thin line of stuffing in the middle of the leaf, keeping the sides empty, and fold the sides toward the center. Then start rolling from the bottom of the leaf to the tip. Each roll must be tight enough for it to cook without spilling its stuffing, which makes the stuffing quantity somewhat tricky to gauge: Too little will help the leaf roll easily but the result will not be as tasty, and too much will make the roll unfold or break while cooking.

The same stuffing mixture and rolling techniques described in this chapter also work for stuffing all sorts of leaves. Swiss chard (add a handful of split cooked chickpeas to the filling for these) or white cabbage leaves must be trimmed into large rectangular pieces, blanched in boiling water for a minute or two to soften the leaves (a bit longer for cabbage), and then stuffed and simply rolled without folding the sides toward the center.

beef-stuffed zucchini

(koussa mehsheh)

Yield: 4 servings

¾ cup (144 g) short-grain rice

10 ounces (280 g) coarsely
  ground beef

Salt and ground black pepper

Ground cinnamon

15 small zucchini, cored
  (See headnote.)

1 medium yellow onion

2 medium tomatoes

Meat (and rice) stuffed zucchini are a staple of Lebanese home cuisine. Preparing whole zucchini for stuffing is a tricky job; the smaller, the better (look for finger-size zucchini … yes, this exists!), though this makes coring them more difficult. To core the zucchini, you need to cut off the stem end and start emptying the center with a *man'ara*, a long metal utensil (a semicircular-shaped skewer), or the thin long handle of a dessert or drink spoon; the trick is to dig enough so that you end up with a hollow whole zucchini with very thin walls that will hold the maximum amount of stuffing. It will take some practice (and some broken ones) before you achieve a satisfying result. The scooped-out portion of the zucchini makes a perfect filling for an omelet or a stuffing for *fatayer* (pastry pies).

Wash and drain the rice. Combine the rice and beef in a bowl and season with salt, pepper, and cinnamon. Mix until well combined. Stuff the cored zucchini with this mixture so that each zucchini is two-thirds to three-quarters full. The rice will absorb water and swell as it cooks and will break the zucchini if too packed. So use not too little and not too much!

Cut the onion into thick slices and place them in the bottom of the pot. Arrange the zucchini over them. Peel the tomatoes, if desired (blanch them in boiling water for a minute to loosen the skins), cut into big chunks, and add to the pot. Add enough water to cover the zucchini and add salt to the water.

Bring to a boil and then lower the heat and cook for about 1 hour until the zucchini and stuffing are cooked through. Serve hot.

Note:
This stuffing is used for all kinds of hollowed-out vegetables—eggplant, potatoes, tomatoes, green peppers—or rolled ones, such as grape leaves, cabbage leaves, and Swiss chard leaves. In the stuffed-leaves version, loads of garlic slices are added to the pot between the layers of stuffed leaves. In the cabbage version, a topping is added consisting of pounded garlic and dried mint, sautéed in butter or olive oil and added at the end of cooking. These are all delicious smells to fill the house!

eggplant fatteh
(fatteh makdouss)

Yield: 4 servings

---

20 eggplants (small ones, preferably finger size; about 2 ¼ pounds, or 1 kg)

6 medium yellow onions

Vegetable oil, as needed

2 ¼ pounds (1 kg) coarsely ground beef

2 tablespoons (40 g) debs el remmen (pomegranate molasses)

1 tablespoon (16 g) red chile paste

½ teaspoon 7 spices (see page 125)

Salt and ground black pepper

1 ½ cups (205 g) pine nuts

2 tablespoons (32 g) tomato paste

5 medium tomatoes

3 pitas

1 garlic clove

1 ¼ cups (290 g) thick yogurt

Vegetables with a meat-only stuffing represent a fancy Sunday meal in all its forms: *koussa ablama*, stuffed zucchini; *sheikh el mehshi*, stuffed eggplants (both served with rice); or other versions of stuffed eggplants, such as this one.

Fatteh comes from *fatta*, meaning "break," as in breaking the grilled bread of the fatteh. Fatteh is a staple souk breakfast, originally a Damascene specialty: a yogurt sauce (made with a hint of garlic and some tahini that will soften the yogurt's taste) and "broken" grilled bread over cooked chickpeas, cubed eggplant, beef tongue, mutton feet (!) … or over stuffed eggplant. The latter version is a fancy party meal rather than a breakfast. The combination of melting eggplant, spicy meat, velvety red sauce, fresh yogurt, and crispy bread is just a taste of heaven!

Makdouss is mainly known as a dish of pickled eggplants stuffed with walnuts, garlic, and chile flakes, preserved in olive oil. This version of fatteh has nothing to do with the pickled version, however; its only similarity is that the eggplants are as small and are also stuffed.

Coring eggplants is much easier than coring zucchini, as the eggplants are firmer and have a tougher skin, making coring a much easier chore!

Cut off the stem ends of the eggplants, scoop out the cores, rinse, and let drain.

Finely chop 2 of the onions. Heat ¼ cup (120 ml) of vegetable oil in a skillet over medium heat and sauté the onions till translucent. Add the ground beef, stir well and then add the molasses, chile paste, 7 spices, and salt and pepper, and stir to break up the meat, cooking until it starts losing its pink color.

Meanwhile, in a small skillet, sauté the pine nuts in a small amount of vegetable oil till light gold. Add half of the pine nuts to the meat mixture. Reserve the remaining pine nuts. Stuff the eggplants with the meat mixture, filling them well with the stuffing, as the meat will shrink a little while it cooks.

Heat ½ cup (120 ml) vegetable oil in a deep skillet over medium heat and cook the stuffed eggplants till lightly browned on the outside. Drain on paper towels.

Thinly slice the remaining 4 onions. In a pot over medium heat, sauté the onions in ¼ cup (60 ml) of vegetable oil until melting and lightly colored.

Add the tomato paste and keep stirring to dissolve it well with the onions. Finely chop the tomatoes and add them to the onions. Raise the heat and boil for 5 minutes. Add the stuffed eggplant to the sauce; there must be enough liquid to just cover the stuffed eggplants. If needed, add water to cover. Bring back to a boil and then lower the heat and cook for about1 ½ hours until the eggplants are well cooked and the sauce is thick. Don't stir much, as the cooked eggplants are very fragile and will break easily.

Meanwhile, cut the pitas into small squares and toast in the oven. Pound the garlic clove into a paste and combine with the yogurt in a bowl.

To assemble, heat a serving dish and start with a layer of stuffed eggplant, loads of thick cooking sauce on top, a layer of toasted bread, some yogurt, and the reserved pine nuts to finish! Serve straight away before the bread gets soggy.

fried taro with chickpeas and onions

(kelkass b tehineh)

Yield: 4 servings

---

1 cup (200 g) dried chickpeas

2 ¼ pounds (1 kg) taro root

Vegetable oil, for frying

5 medium yellow onions

5 tablespoons (75 ml) olive oil

½ cup (120 g) tahini

Juice of 4 lemons

Salt

Kelkass (Colocasia esculenta) is one of those weird old vegetables that you may not know how to use. Still, its plant is the most gracious ever, with large, light green leaves called elephant ears (if ever someone happens to see the plant!). The taro itself is the root, the tuber, with a dark brown and hairy exterior and a hard, white starchy flesh. It is hard to peel and stains the hands deep red and makes them itchy. So peel with care ... and use gloves! Taro root, or taro potato, is a common ingredient in African, Oceanic, Indian, and Japanese cuisines—which makes it easy to find in specialized groceries. Serve this dish with bread and radishes.

Soak the chickpeas in water to cover for at least 10 hours. Drain before proceeding.

Peel the taro root (wearing plastic kitchen gloves) and cut into big chunks. Wash well, drain, and pat dry. Heat a deep pot or deep fryer with several inches of vegetable oil and deep-fry the taro until lightly colored all over. Drain on paper towels.

Cut the onions into thin slices. Heat the olive oil in a large skillet over medium heat and sauté the onions until they start to color, about 15 minutes. Add the chickpeas and 1 cup (235 ml) water and cook over a low heat until the chickpeas are cooked but still a bit firm. Add the fried taro and cook for 30 more minutes.

Meanwhile, mix the tahini and lemon juice. Add to the taro when well cooked. Season to taste with salt, bring to a boil, and let it boil for 20 minutes so that the sauce thicken and coats the taro pieces. Serve at room temperature.

taro with lentils

(kelkass bi adass)

Yield: 4 servings

———

2 ¼ pounds (1 kg) taro root

Vegetable oil, for frying

5 medium yellow onions

5 tablespoons (75 ml) olive oil

1 cup (192 g) small brown lentils

2 to 4 tablespoons (12 to 24 g)
 ground sumac

2 garlic cloves

Salt

½ of a bunch of mint or 2
 tablespoons (3 g) dried mint

Another version of taro root is made with lentils. As in so many cases, there are two camps of preference: those who cook it with tahini and those who cook it without. The combination of taro and lentils is very earthy and made refreshing by the acidity of sumac water … all mountain ingredients and tastes!

Sumac water does not mean sumac powder diluted in water. The purists prefer not to grind sumac (a grinder is not an easy utensil to find in a simple mountain kitchen). Instead, they keep it as it comes, in whole berries, and soak the whole berries overnight in just enough water to cover. The next day, they rub the berries well in the water, and the result is a very deep velvet red water with a tangy sumac taste. However, you aren't likely to find sumac berries available commercially, so you will have to replace them with a good-quality sumac powder!

Peel the taro root (wearing plastic kitchen gloves) and cut into big chunks. Wash well, drain, and pat dry. Heat a deep pot or deep fryer with several inches of vegetable oil and deep-fry the taro until light golden. Drain on paper towels.

Cut the onions into thin slices. Heat the olive oil in a large skillet over medium heat and sauté the onions until they start to color, about 15 minutes. Add the lentils and 1 cup (235 ml) water and let cook over low heat. Lentils are quick to cook and will take less than 30 minutes.

When the lentils are cooked, add the fried taro and the sumac and let cook for 30 minutes.

Crush the garlic cloves into a paste with ½ teaspoon of salt, add the fresh or dried mint and crush again, and add to the taro and lentils. Season to taste with salt and let it all cook for 5 minutes longer. Serve warm.

eggplant in spicy tomato sauce

(massaee't batenjenn)

Yield: 4 servings

———————

½ cup (100 g) dried chickpeas

3 ¼ pounds (1.5 kg) large eggplant

6 tablespoons (90 ml) olive oil

Salt

3 medium yellow onions

1 fresh red or green chile pepper

1 head of garlic, cloves separated
   and peeled

2 ¼ pounds (1 kg) tomatoes

Massaa' means "cold," and you might wonder if this dish has this name because it is eaten cold or because the name and the dish resembles the Greek moussaka (minus the meat). We say that to prepare *massaee't batenjenn* is to praise eggplants because it is the best way to cook them, where they melt in the sweet tomato sauce. It is said that there are as many eggplant recipes as there are days of the year and that a good cook must be able to do a new recipe every day!

———————

Preheat the oven to 400°F (200°C, or gas mark 6).

Soak the chickpeas overnight in water to cover. Drain, place in a saucepan, add water to cover, and bring to a boil. Lower the heat and simmer until cooked.

Peel the eggplant, cut into big chunks, sprinkle with 2 tablespoons (28 ml) of the olive oil and some salt, and rub well to coat the eggplant. Spread on a baking sheet and bake until the pieces start coloring, about 20 minutes.

Cut the onions into slices and chop the chile pepper. Heat the remaining 4 tablespoons (60 ml) olive oil in a large skillet over medium heat and sauté the onions until translucent.

Add the peeled whole garlic cloves and the chile pepper. Add the cooked chickpeas.

Peel the tomatoes, if desired (blanch them in boiling water for a minute to loosen the skins), cut into big chunks, and add to the skillet. Bring to a boil and then lower the heat and cook for 20 minutes or until the sauce starts to thicken. Add the baked eggplant pieces, season with salt, and cook for 20 minutes more. Serve at room temperature.

summer zucchini stew

(mfaraket koussa)

Yield: 4 servings

————

1 cup (200 g) dried chickpeas

1 ¾ pounds (795 g) yellow onions

1 fresh red or green chile pepper

¼ cup (60 ml) olive oil

4 garlic cloves, peeled

2 ¼ pounds (1 kg) zucchini

¼ teaspoon ground allspice

¼ teaspoon ground white pepper

Salt

2 ¼ pounds (1 kg) tomatoes

Prepared in an easy style, this is one of the easiest and simplest summer stews for taking advantage of the abundant summer zucchini. Lebanese zucchini are light green and small—the smaller, the better, mainly to use for *mehsheh*, stuffed vegetables (meaty or meatless versions).

Soak the chickpeas overnight in water to cover. Drain, place in a saucepan, add water to cover, and bring to a boil. Lower the heat and simmer until cooked.

Thinly slice the onions and chop the chile pepper. Heat the olive oil in a large skillet over medium heat and sauté the onions, whole garlic cloves, and chile pepper until the onions turn translucent, about 15 minutes.

Cut the zucchini into cubes, add to the onions, and sauté until the zucchini pieces start coloring, about 10 minutes. Season with the allspice, white pepper, and salt to taste.

Peel the tomatoes, if desired (blanch them in boiling water for a minute to loosen the skins), finely chop, and add to the zucchini. Add the chickpeas, stir, and cook the stew over low heat for 30 minutes. Serve at room temperature.

wilted greens with fried onions

(hendbeh b zeit)

Hendbeh b zeit is a mezze table must! Traditionally, the bitter, dark green leaves of wild dandelion are required. But substitutes are easy: Kale or Swiss chard are as good as dandelion greens, or try any kind of dark, bitter greens. Just follow the recipe!

Yield: 4 servings

---

2 ¼ pounds (1 kg) dandelion greens (or kale or Swiss chard)

Vegetable oil, for frying

2 medium yellow onions

2 garlic cloves

¼ cup (60 ml) olive oil

1 bunch of green coriander, stalks and leaves separated

Salt

Juice of 1 lemon

Bring a pot of water to a boil. Coarsely chop the dandelion greens and drop it, in batches, into the boiling water for 3 minutes. Drain and then squeeze well to get out most of the water.

Heat about 1 inch (2.5 cm) of vegetable oil in a deep skillet over medium heat. Cut 1 of the onions into slices and fry them in the vegetable oil until golden and crispy. Drain on paper towels.

Finely chop the remaining onion and the garlic. Heat the olive oil in a large skillet over medium heat and sauté the onion and garlic in the oil. Chop the coriander stalks and add to the skillet. When the onion is melting and starting to color, add the blanched dandelion greens, stir well, raise the heat, and let it all cook and dry out for 5 minutes. Season to taste with salt.

Chop the coriander leaves and add to the dandelion greens. Add the lemon juice (you may need more than 1 lemon, depending on your taste). Serve hot or at room temperature.

stuffed artichokes

(ardeh chawkeh mehsheh)

Yield: 6 servings

———

2 medium potatoes

2 medium carrots

18 pearl onions (or 1 large white onion)

3 tablespoons (45 ml) olive oil

7 ounces (200 g) green peas

6 large artichoke, trimmed down to edible hearts

Juice of 2 lemons

½ teaspoon salt

Artichokes are from the wonderful plant that is related to the gracious antique acanthus leaves that adorned Roman Corinthian capitals scattered all over Baalbeck and other Roman temples and ruins in Lebanon. From the thistle family, the artichoke hides its delicious, sweet "heart" behind hard leaves and thorns! So trimming and preparing it is a bit of a chore, but the rest of the preparation is very easy and fast.

Peel the potatoes, carrots, and onions. If using pearl onions, keep whole; if using 1 large onion, thinly slice it. Dice the potatoes and carrots into small cubes.

Cover the bottom of a pan with the olive oil. Add the onions and cover with the carrots, potatoes, green peas, and end with the artichoke hearts on top. Add ½ cup (120 ml) water, put it on to boil, and then lower the heat and let it cook for 40 minutes or until the vegetables are tender.

Season with the lemon juice and salt. Let it cook for 5 more minutes. If the sauce is too runny, mash some potato cubes and stir to thicken it.

Set up the artichoke hearts in a dish, fill them with the vegetables (or rather, mound the stuffing on top), and drizzle with the sauce. Serve at room temperature.

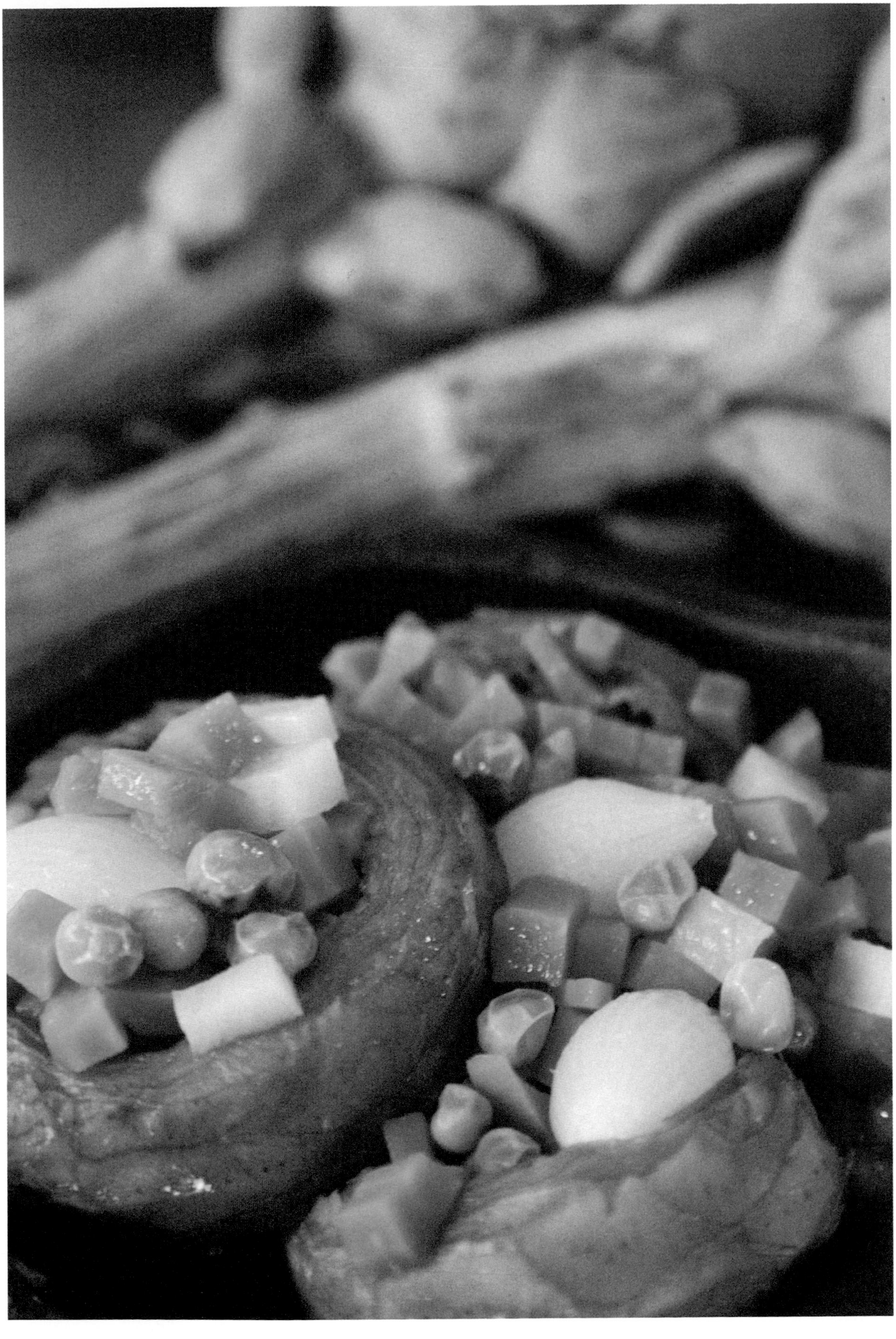

fried cauliflower with tarator sauce

(arnabit meeleh + tarator)

I believe that cauliflower expresses itself best when fried! It is just a yummy taste, with a contrast between the crisp florets and the soft stalks. It goes perfectly with tarator, the thin, white, lemony tahini sauce that counterbalances the fried aspect.

Yield: 4 servings

———

For the tarator:
1 garlic clove
Salt
½ cup (120 g) tahini
Juice of 2 lemons
1 tablespoon (15 ml) olive oil

For the cauliflower:
1 large head of cauliflower
Vegetable oil, for frying
Salt

To prepare the tarator, crush the garlic finely with a bit of salt and add to the tahini in a bowl. Add the lemon juice little by little to the tahini—at first it will thicken and turn very hard, but enough lemon juice should be added to obtain a runny consistency (this may be more than 2 lemons). Season to taste with salt and blend in the olive oil.

To prepare the cauliflower, divide it into florets about the size of Ping-Pong balls (too small and they will be dry; too big and they will not crisp up enough). Heat vegetable oil in a deep pot over medium-high heat. Deep-fry the cauliflower in the hot oil, in batches, until golden. Drain on paper towels. Season to taste with salt and serve hot with the tarator.

fried zucchini and eggplant

(koussa w batenjenn mee'leh)

Yield: 4 servings

———

18 ounces (510 g) eggplant

18 ounces (510 g) zucchini

Salt

Vegetable oil, for frying

3 garlic cloves

2 tablespoons (28 ml) red wine vinegar or cider vinegar

2 tablespoons (40 g) debs el remmen (pomegranate molasses)

Everything is better from a fryer! This is especially true for zucchini, which gets crispy, and eggplant, which turns soft and melting. Fried vegetables are a summer treat (even if not so adapted to the temperature!), as vegetables are abundant and have a bit less water in them from the hot sun and they crisp up and color better when fried.

———

Half peel (in bands) the eggplant. Slice the eggplant and the zucchini into strips about ¾ inch (2 cm) thick.

Lay the strips out on a tray, season generously with salt, and let sit for a while so they can exude their water. (Traditionally they were laid out in the hot sun.) Dry them well with paper towels so that they do not spatter in the hot oil.

Heat vegetable oil in a deep pot over medium-high heat or in a deep fryer. First fry the zucchini until golden brown on both sides. Drain on paper towels. Then fry the eggplant until golden brown on both sides. Drain on paper towels. (Fry the zucchini before the eggplant because the eggplant will change the taste of the oil.)

Crush the garlic and divide in half. Mix one half with the vinegar and drizzle over the fried zucchini.

Mix the rest of the garlic with the pomegranate molasses and drizzle over the fried eggplant. Serve straight away.

fried eggplant with yogurt

(mfassah')

Yield: 4 servings

———————

2 large eggplants (18 ounces,
   or 510 g, or more each)

Salt

Vegetable oil, for frying

1 garlic clove

2 cups + 3 tablespoons (490 g) yogurt

Very thick slices of deep-fried eggplant, contrasting between a crisp surface and a soft heart, are soaked in fresh, cold laban (yogurt) with a hint of garlic. Fried goes refreshing! *Mfassah'* means "torn apart" or "separated," as the eggplant is torn apart before adding the yogurt, so that the yogurt soaks into it well. *Mfassah'* is traditionally served with *kebbeh bel sanyieh* (kibbeh pie).

———————

Half peel (in bands) the eggplants. Cut into thick slices, lay out on a tray, season generously with salt, and let sit for a while to exude some of its water. Dry them well with paper towels so that they do no spatter in the hot oil.

Heat vegetable oil in a deep pot over medium heat or in a deep fryer. Fry the eggplant slices, in batches, long enough for the eggplant to nearly burn, partly so that the thick slices cook all the way through and partly because the dark deep-frying will create a wonderful flavor to contrast with the fresh laban. Drain on paper towels.

Crush the garlic clove and mix it with the yogurt. Put the eggplant in a serving dish, tearing the slices a bit, and drown them with the garlicky yogurt.

potatoes with green coriander and chile flakes

(batata harra)

Coriander and garlic are a classic combination in Lebanese cuisine … and a perfect match! Often, the mixture is sautéed before adding it to a recipe, and this smell is typical of a home Lebanese kitchen.

Batata harra means literally "hot potato" (as in spicy), as it is fried potato (baked in some lighter versions!) that is seasoned with the coriander-garlic power combination and hot pepper, or red chile flakes. *Batata harra* is a must for a mezze table.

Yield: 4 servings

———

3 potatoes

3 tablespoons (45 ml) olive oil

Salt

1 bunch of green coriander

2 garlic cloves

Juice of 1 lemon

Crushed red chile flakes

Preheat the oven to 500°F (250°C, or gas mark 10).

Peel the potatoes and cut into big cubes. Drizzle with the olive oil and season to taste with salt, rubbing well so that all the pieces are coated with oil and salt. Put on a baking sheet and bake for 40 minutes, or longer, until puffed and golden.

Meanwhile, finely the chop coriander, crush the garlic with a little salt, and mix them all together with the lemon juice. Add red chile flakes to taste. Transfer the potatoes to a serving plate, pour the dressing over top, mix well, and serve hot.

chard stalks in tarator

(dlou' selee' mtaballeh)

Yield: 4 servings

---

20 Swiss chard stalks

1 garlic clove

Salt

½ cup (120 g) tahini

Juice of 2 lemons

1 tablespoon (15 ml) olive oil

Leaves from 2 sprigs of flat-leaf
    parsley

Tarator is an easy-to-prepare sauce that often serves as a dressing, too. It is a perfect accompaniment to baked fish, meat shawarma, or falafel and is a wonderful dressing for boiled potatoes, cooked beans, or *dlou' selee'* (the white stalks of Swiss chard). In a perfect "use it all" approach, when chard leaves are used for stuffed vegetables, the thick watery stalks should also be used for something—in this case, dressed with tarator and served as a dish on its own.

Clean the chard stalks by taking off their top and bottom and stripping any tough strings if the stalks are too big. Bring a lightly salted pot of water to a boil and cook the stalks in the boiling water for 10 minutes or until the stalks are tender. Drain and let cool.

Crush the garlic finely with a bit of salt and add to the tahini in a bowl.

Add the lemon juice little by little to the tahini—at first it will thicken and turn very hard, but enough lemon juice should be added to obtain a runny consistency (this may be more than 2 lemons). Season to taste with salt and blend in the olive oil.

Cut the chard stalks into pieces and drizzle the thick tarator over them. Decorate with parsley leaves and serve.

potatoes with coriander and cumin

(batata jezzinyieh)

Batata jezzynyieh is the town of Jezzine's take on *batata harra*, but made with cumin, the South's spice. The joke goes that a guest, over lunch in the South, tasted cumin in every single dish he ate and so handed back his water to the host, asking her if she was not mistaken by serving him "un-cumined" water!

Yield: 4 servings

---

3 medium potatoes
5 tablespoons (75 ml) olive oil
Salt
1 garlic clove
⅓ of a bunch of green coriander
½ teaspoon ground cumin
Juice of 1 lemon

Preheat the oven to 500°F (250°C, or gas mark 10).

Cut the potatoes into thick wedges, without peeling them. Drizzle with 2 tablespoons (28 ml) of the olive oil, season to taste with salt, and rub well for the pieces to be coated with oil and salt. Put on a baking sheet and bake for 40 minutes, or longer, until puffed and golden.

Crush the garlic clove with a little salt. Chop the coriander and crush it with the garlic until you obtain a smooth paste. Add the cumin, lemon juice, and the remaining olive oil and drizzle the mixture over the cooked potatoes while still on the baking sheet. If the potatoes stick to the pan, let them soak in the cumin sauce for a couple of minutes and they will detach. Serve warm.

mashed potatoes with herbs

(batata melee'yieh)

In kibbeh country, Ehden and Zgharta, potato doesn't have its kibbeh form (as elsewhere), but rather is prepared as *melee'-yieh*, or mashed and seasoned with herbs. It's similar to potato kibbeh, but without the bulgur.

Yield: 4 servings

———————

3 medium potatoes

2 scallions

2 sprigs of mint

Salt and ground white pepper

Olive oil

Bring a pot of water to a boil and boil the potatoes until tender. Peel and mash finely with a fork, a potato masher, a potato ricer, or in a food mill. Never use an electric mixer, as the potatoes will turn gluey.

Finely chop the scallions and mint and add to the mashed potato. Season to taste with salt and white pepper (white so as not to "stain" the potato!).

Add 2 tablespoons (28 ml) olive oil, mix well, and serve topped with a generous drizzle of olive oil.

SALADS AND BREADS

Salads are an important part of the meal in Lebanon and not considered just an optional side. An everyday meal starts with a salad, followed by a stew, served with rice or bulgur. Salads are typically composed of available, fresh, seasonal herbs and vegetables. Romaine lettuce is a winter staple, as are many herbs, mainly wild ones. And summer is tomato time and again, served with fragrant herbs.

TABOULEH:
A NATIONAL SYMBOL

It's difficult to adequately describe what tabouleh means to Lebanese cuisine. It's not just any dish, and it's definitely not just a salad! Not a Sunday dinner, nor a mezze table, nor any celebratory meal of any kind can get started without a tabouleh.

In an article about tabouleh for Lebanon's first National Tabouleh Day, Dr. Antoine Daher compared it to Lebanon: a mix of diverse ingredients, where one can distinguish every single one but can never separate one from another. It's just like this country, made of such diversity and differences, all very distinguishable but never separable!

Everyone has his or her own version of tabouleh, and everyone naturally believes that their version (or their mother's version) is the best tabouleh ever. There are those who like it without bulgur, and those who like it with loads. Should it be cracking-hard bulgur or soaked and softened? Very lemony or not? With sharab el hosrom (verjus) or not? Chopped micro-fine or not? There are endless versions!

Tabouleh is—or traditionally was—a seasonal dish. Each home had its own maskabeh: a plot of land to grow flat-leaf parsley and mint. Later, with urbanization, the maskabeh became a pot kept on the balcony in the city. Springtime brings the heat, flowers, good weather ... and fresh products, like parsley. Spring days are thus the best time to enjoy tabouleh. Now that, alas, there are no longer seasonal products (parsley and mint—and all the rest—can be found all year round), we Lebanese still wait for the good mountain parsley (baladi parsley) in order to make really excellent tabouleh. The first jammeh (harvest or cutting), which used to be a kind of ritual, traditionally yields the best parsley: tender, fresh, and flavorsome.

The whole tabouleh-making process is a ritual. First you must trim the parsley, making bunches as large as the palm of your hand. This is the typical Sunday morning ritual: going to pick parsley and a little mint, and sitting in the long-awaited spring sunshine (with a straw hat!) to clean the parsley and strip off the mint leaves. Then you must wash the bunches and leave them to dry before you chop them.

There is only one way to chop the parsley: finely. Hold the bunch tightly under the palm of your hand on the chopping board and chop with a sharp knife. The blade should cut the parsley just once, never twice; otherwise, it will be fine, certainly, but it will lose its juiciness and will blacken and appear crushed. In other words, the parsley should be sliced rather than chopped. So some skill is required, and this can only be acquired with time and practice. Then the mint: Pick some leaves, chop them finely, and put them under a little of the chopped parsley in the bowl, so they do not turn black.

Tabouleh is eaten with pieces of romaine lettuce or white cabbage, or, in season, tender grape leaves. Regardless of the many variations, tabouleh is mainly made of finely chopped flat-leaf parsley, a bit of mint, scallions, tomato, and bulgur. It has nothing to do with couscous, quinoa, cucumber, or shrimps—or any of those different Western variations and ingredients!

tabouleh

Yield: 4 servings

————————

2 medium tomatoes

2 tablespoons (20 g) fine-grind bulgur

½ of a bunch of mint

1 fresh green chile pepper

4 bunches of flat-leaf parsley

½ of a bunch of scallions

¼ teaspoon ground black pepper

Salt

Juice of 2 lemons

6 tablespoons (90 ml) olive oil

Romaine lettuce leaves,
    white cabbage leaves,
    or fresh grape leaves,
    for serving

For the record, I like my tabouleh lemony, with a note of hot green chile pepper, transforming each mouthful into a fresh hit of flavor on a hot summer day. I start with the tomato, diced into tiny cubes and mixed with the bulgur so it soaks up the tomato juices. Then I very finely chop the scallions (true spring onions are the best, if you can get them) and rub them with some salt and pepper to soften their crunch.

————————————————————

Finely dice the tomatoes, place in a large bowl, and add the bulgur. Stir so that the bulgur is well mixed with the tomatoes and soaks up their juice.

Chop the mint and chile pepper and add to the bowl. Finely slice the parsley and add to the bowl, covering up the mint to prevent it from turning black. Finely chop the scallions, sprinkle with the pepper and a bit of salt, and rub a bit with the fingertips, so the scallions soften. Add to the bowl. Do not stir!

Do not mix the tabouleh until ready to serve. Start mixing with a spoon and a hand, to be sure the tabouleh is well mixed, and then add the lemon juice and olive oil. Season to taste with salt. A tabouleh should not be dry, but it should not be soupy either. Serve straight away, with romaine lettuce, white cabbage, or fresh grape leaves … a tabouleh does not wait!

TEN COMMANDMENTS
OF TABOULEH

1. Tabouleh is a parsley salad.
2. Only flat-leaf parsley is used.
3. Only bulgur is used.
4. Green onions or dry white onions only are used.
5. Ingredients must be chopped by hand.
6. Ingredients must specifically be sliced and not randomly chopped.
7. The mint must be sliced quickly so it does not blacken.
8. Olive oil is the only oil used.
9. Tabouleh is mixed and seasoned only at the last minute before serving.
10. A hit of flavor is a must—too lemony and a bit hot is never too much!

JEZZINE'S TAKE ON TABOULEH

Jezzine is a town that is very **well** known for its refreshing weather, impressive cascades, and nearby amazing pine tree **forest** in Bkassine. Typical local specialties are **shmamitt b' laban** (fried eggs in yogurt) and **kebbeh** jezzinyieh (bell-shaped kibbeh filled **with** strained yogurt and ground meat), and their **own** version of tabouleh, taboulet el hommos, the chickpea tabouleh. Split chickpeas are soaked for around 10 hours, long enough for them to be tender enough to be eaten raw, and so replace the bulgur in the tabouleh. If split chickpeas are not available, soak regular (whole) chickpeas long enough for them to get tender (24 hours) and then put them in a kitchen towel and crush and rub, which will split the chickpeas and take off the outer peel at the same time.

purslane and beets

(baa'leh w shmandar)

Yield: 4 servings

---

18 ounces (510 g) beets

2 bunches of purslane

Juice of ½ of a lemon

1 tablespoon (15 ml) red wine vinegar

3 tablespoons (45 ml) olive oil

Salt

Baa'leh (purslane) is a secret herb of Lebanese cuisine. Its "meaty" leaves, "iron-y" taste, and dark green color make it very special. The closest you can get to purslane (if you can't find it) is watercress (watercress is more watery, more fragile, and less flavorful). The best *baa'leh* is the wild one that covers the orchards in early spring—its smaller leaves are a concentrate of what *baa'leh* is! The beets are a perfect companion to purslane, complementing the green with their deep red color and sweet flavor.

Boil the beets in a medium pot with enough water to cover until cooked and tender (which takes about an hour). Let cool, then peel, cut into chunks, and place in a bowl. Add the purslane, tearing the leaves into pieces.

Prepare the dressing by mixing the lemon juice, vinegar, olive oil, and salt to taste. Drizzle over the purslane and beets and serve.

bread salad

(fattoush)

1 pita

2 medium tomatoes

7 ounces (200 g) radishes

2 scallions

7 ounces (200 g) arugula, torn

½ of a bunch of purslane, torn

½ of a bunch of thyme

½ of a bunch of flat-leaf parsley

½ of a bunch of mint

1 tablespoon (6 g) ground sumac

1 tablespoon (20 g) debs el remmen
(pomegranate molasses)

¼ cup (60 ml) olive oil

Salt

Fattoush comes from Arabic *fatta*, meaning "break," from breaking the grilled Arabic bread (pita) over the fattoush. If you've ever heard of the Montagues and the Capulets, it is the same as with fattoush and tabouleh! There is a constant dilemma of choosing between one and the other for a mezze … or maybe just go for both.

If tabouleh is all about fine chopping and dicing, fattoush is the converse, with big chunks of vegetables and fragrant herbs from the garden. Some like it with a hint of crushed garlic and a tangier sauce with lemon juice; this is up to personal taste. Still, some rules are de rigueur: It isn't a fattoush without purslane, without grilled bread, and without sumac.

Grill the pita on a stovetop grill pan or toast it.

Cut the tomatoes into chunks, slice the radishes, and coarsely chop the scallions. Tear the arugula and purslane into pieces. Strip the leaves from the thyme and chop the parsley and mint.

Mix the chopped vegetables, arugula, purslane, thyme, parsley, and mint in a large bowl. Mix in the sumac, pomegranate molasses, and olive oil and season to taste with salt. Break the grilled bread into bite-size pieces over it all and serve straight away.

A BOWL FOR BEANS

Beit Chabab is a village that is historically renowned for its beautiful traditional architecture and handicrafts, especially for its pottery, though the tradition has unfortunately declined in recent years. Typical forms were of large olive oil jars, water jars, mortars, olive jars, big bowls to knead bread dough or keshek... and a special bowl just for bean salad (mainly red beans, though the White Bean Salad could be prepared in such a bowl)—a dark-colored, hard bowl (similar to Japanese raku pottery) that is used to prepare bean salads from A to Z. First you pound the garlic, then mix it with olive oil and lemon juice, and finish with the warm cooked beans. The porous pottery absorbs the flavors of the garlic, olive oil, and beans, and the salads made in the pot become even better year after year!

PASTRY

Mouaa'janat are pastries that used to be prepared on "baking day," when bread was baked at home every 10 or 14 days. And as mothers were busy baking on that day, lunch had to be simple and built around the same dough used for the bread: spread as a pizza with za'atar or cheese sprinkled over it or folded into a pie filled with vegetables (purslane or spinach), keshek (dried fermented yogurt and bulgur), or a meat mixture.

white bean salad

(fassolia aa'rida moutabale)

Yield: 4 servings

————

1 ¼ cups (220 g) large flat dried
   white beans, butter beans, or lima
   beans

1 garlic clove

Salt

Juice of 1 lemon

¼ cup (60 ml) olive oil

Leaves from 2 sprigs of flat-leaf
   parsley

Fassolia (from the Latin *faseolus*) means "beans" and *aa'rida* means "large," so this recipe refers to flat, large white beans that grow on a vine that covers big parts of the garden. A single plant grows indefinitely. The beans are picked green in August and are tender and fast-cooking. Tender *fassolia aa'rida* is a delicacy that needs short cooking over a low fire and gives plump, pearl white, melting beans that are best served warm with a drizzle of lemon and olive oil … they are not called butter beans for nothing!

Salt should never be added to the cooking water for beans, as it will toughen the beans and they will not cook well.

———————————

Boil the beans in enough water to cover over low heat until softened and cooked through. Lower the heat a little before the beans are completely soft, as they will continue to cook in the liquid.

Drain the warm, soft beans. Crush the garlic together with a pinch of salt, add the lemon juice, olive oil, and more salt to taste, and drizzle the dressing over the beans. Sprinkle the parsley leaves over the beans and serve warm.

thyme flatbread

(manaiish)

Yield: 4 servings

For the dough:

½ teaspoon active dry yeast

¼ teaspoon sugar

2 cups (240 g) whole wheat flour

¼ cup (60 ml) olive oil

1 teaspoon salt

For the spread:

Za'atar

Olive oil

The ultimate breakfast, a *manousheh* (plural *manaiish*) is a flatbread, a pizza-like pie, covered with za'atar (thyme, sesame seeds, sumac, and salt) mixed with oil and baked in the oven or over a *saj*, which is a concave steel plaque with fire beneath it and the flatbread cooks on the top. Its distinctive smell is typical of an early-morning mountain breakfast.

The flatbread goes well with some sliced tomato and cucumber and mint sprigs. Roll it all up and bite into a healthy breakfast. These *manaiish* are around 12 inches (30 cm) in diameter, but they can also be prepared as small bites, less than 4 inches (10 cm) in diameter.

To prepare the dough, dissolve the yeast and the sugar in ½ cup (120 ml) lukewarm water (too cold and the yeast will not be active and rise; too hot and it will be killed). It should rise and double its amount or more, taking about 10 minutes.

Mix well the flour with the olive oil, so that every grain is coated with oil. Add the yeast mixture, salt, and enough warm water to form a dough. Add ½ cup (120 ml) at a time and knead well, so the dough doesn't turn loose and liquid. The dough should be elastic enough and not stick to the hands or the bowl. Shape it into a ball and let it rest for at least 3 hours, covered, in a warm place, for the dough to rise to double its original volume.

Preheat the oven to 400°F (200°C, or gas mark 6).

Flour your hands and divide the dough. For individual regular-size manousheh, divide the dough into tennis ball–size pieces, roll into rounds, and sprinkle with flour. For nibble-size breads, divide the dough into big pieces, roll out thin, and cut out 4-inch (10 cm) disks with a cookie cutter (or a glass). Re-roll the dough to use it all and arrange the rounds on a baking sheet.

Mix the za'atar with enough olive oil to obtain a semi-thick, spreadable consistency. Spread the za'atar mixture over the dough.

Bake individual-size manousheh for about 15 minutes until golden. Bake nibble-size manousheh on a baking sheet for around 10 minutes until the bread is baked and the border starts coloring.

cheese pies

(fatayer jebneh)

Yield: 4 servings

————

For the dough:
½ teaspoon active dry yeast
¼ teaspoon sugar
2 cups (240 g) whole wheat flour
¼ cup (60 ml) olive oil
1 teaspoon salt

For the filling:
18 ounces (510 g) akkawi cheese
(or substitute half mozzarella and
half Gruyère or other good melting
cheese)
1 medium yellow onion
1 medium tomato

Called *samboussek* (for small individual semicircular pieces), or *manoushet jebneh* (for big pizza-pie ones), these cheese flatbreads are made in Lebanon with a special kind of cheese, *akkawi* (from the Palestinian city of Akka) as we call it in Lebanon, which is a white cheese that melts well. So look for a "melting" white cheese that is not very watery or else the bread will never bake and crisp up properly. This version of *fatayer jebneh* is a little fancier, with onion for the taste and tomato for the color, but they can also be made with just cheese.

————

To make the dough, dissolve the yeast and the sugar in ½ cup (120 ml) lukewarm water (too cold and the yeast will not be active and rise; too hot and it will be killed). It should rise and double its amount or more, taking about 10 minutes.

Mix well the flour with the olive oil, so that every grain is coated with oil. Add the yeast mixture, salt, and enough warm water to form a dough. Add ½ cup (120 ml) at a time and knead well, so the dough doesn't turn loose and liquid. The dough should be elastic enough and not stick to the hands or the bowl. Shape it into a ball and let it rest for at least 3 hours, covered, in a warm place, for the dough to rise to double its original volume.

Preheat the oven to 400°F (200°C, or gas mark 6).

To make the filling, coarsely grate the cheese into a bowl. Finely chop the onion and add to the cheese. Dice the tomato and add to the cheese. Mix well; there should be no need to salt the mixture, as the cheese is salty enough.

Roll the dough out thinly and cut out small disks (4 inches, or 10 cm, in diameter). Put 1 tablespoon (15 g) of the filling in the middle of it. You may leave the disks flat (spread out the filling if you do this), or you may fold the disks in two, like a turnover, and seal the border by pinching it. Arrange on a baking sheet and bake for 10 to 15 minutes until lightly golden.

BREADS

Bread is a main component of a Lebanese meal and the basis of the diet. It has a religious significance for Christians and has sacred values for all. "Bread" is khobz in Arabic or aiish, which means "life" too. One cannot throw bread or allow a piece of it to be on the floor. Saying that two people shared "bread and salt" is expressing the strongest bonds between them. Bread baking is (or used to be) part of women's affairs, as they are traditionally the feeders and nourishers of the family. The art of bread making is passed down from mother to daughter, and the best bakers are very proud of their skills.

Bread used to be made from whole wheat flour, often mixed with a bit of corn grit (flour) or oat or other cereals, and leavened with sourdough. Today it is mainly made from white flour. There are several types of traditional breads.

Pita bread is what we call "Arabic bread" (khobz forn, "oven bread," or khobz el souk, "souk bread," as opposed to home bread) and is the main one consumed nowadays. Baked in industrial ovens, it has two layers, is thinner and softer than tortillas, and can be around 12 inches (30 cm) in diameter.

Saj bread is the thinnest, a single layer, baked on a convex steel sheet, and is nearly 2 feet (60 cm) in diameter!

Tabouneh and tannour ovens are similar to the Indian tandoor oven (hence the name) and are clay ovens, built either in the ground or on it. Tannour bread is smaller and thicker than saj. Tabouneh bread is even smaller and has two layers and is somewhat similar to Arabic bread.

Bread is an eating tool: It is cut into small squares and used as a lee'meh (a "shovel-bite," or mouthful). One never uses his or her own fork, spoon, or fingers to eat from a communal dish (what one eats with can never be dipped into a communal dish!), but rather a small piece of bread that can be shaped as a small spoon, or shovel, to scoop up hummus, moutabal, or whatever is eaten with bread (similar to using a piece of cabbage or lettuce for a tabouleh).

Bread is also used for sandwiches, of course, with fillings including labneh (strained yogurt), cheese (typically fresh white cheese), and jam (apricot or fig); the filling is spread on the bread, which is then rolled up like a burrito. These are called aa'rouss, which is the same name for a sandwich and for a bride!

spinach and sumac pies

(fatayer khodra)

These herb pies are mainly of spinach, with onion and lemony sumac. An even better version is the *baa'leh* (purslane) pies, which have a very earthy taste. Or try any kind of dark green leaves or herbs, especially sorrel, which has a pleasing sour taste.

Yield: 4 servings

For the dough:

½ teaspoon active dry yeast

¼ teaspoon sugar

2 cups (240 g) whole wheat flour

¼ cup (60 ml) olive oil

1 teaspoon salt

For the filling:

2 ¼ pounds (1 kg) spinach

Salt

1 medium yellow onion

2 tablespoons (12 g) ground sumac

2 tablespoons (28 ml) olive oil

To make the dough, dissolve the yeast and the sugar in ½ cup (120 ml) lukewarm water (too cold and the yeast will not be active and rise; too hot and it will be killed). It should rise and double its amount or more, taking about 10 minutes.

Mix well the flour with the olive oil, so that every grain is coated with oil. Add the yeast mixture, salt, and enough warm water to form a dough. Add ½ cup (120 ml) at a time and knead well so the dough doesn't turn loose and liquid. The dough should be elastic enough and not stick to the hands or the bowl. Shape it into a ball and let it rest for at least 3 hours, covered, in a warm place, for the dough to rise to double its original volume.

To make the filling, chop the spinach, place in a colander, and rub with salt. Keep the spinach in the colander to drain its water for 30 minutes.

Preheat the oven to 400°F (200°C, or gas mark 6).

Squeeze the spinach well to remove additional water and transfer to a bowl. Finely chop the onion, add it to the spinach, and add the sumac and the olive oil. Mix well to obtain a dough-like mixture; you want it to be dry, without excess liquid.

Roll the bread dough out thinly and cut out small disks (4 inches, or 10 cm, in diameter). Put 1 tablespoon (15 g) of the filling in the middle of each disk. Fold one-third of the side in toward the middle, then the other one-third, and then the last part, so as to transform the circle into a folded triangle enclosing the filling. Pinch the borders to seal them and arrange on a baking sheet.

Bake for 10 to 15 minutes until lightly golden. Serve at room temperature.

meat pies

(lahm b'ajin)

Yield: 20 pies

For the dough:

½ teaspoon active dry yeast

½ teaspoon sugar

5 ½ cups (688 g) all-purpose flour

¼ cup (60 ml) vegetable oil

1 teaspoon salt

For the filling:

2 ¼ pounds (1 kg) ground beef

2 ¼ pounds (1 kg) tomatoes

1 ½ pounds (680 g) onions

7 garlic cloves, peeled

1 or 2 fresh green chile peppers
   (optional)

1 tablespoon (16 g) tomato paste

1 tablespoon (16 g) hot chile paste

1 bunch of flat-leaf parsley

1 teaspoon salt

1 teaspoon ground black pepper

For the garnish:

Lemon juice

Paprika

No one does *lahm b'ajin* like an Armenian bakery. A good one must be a paper-thin flatbread, topped with a moist and spicy meat mixture. Traditional preparation involves a procession that starts at the greengrocer, to buy the needed tomato, parsley, onion, garlic, and hot pepper. Then it's off to the butcher, to mince it all together with the meat (you will need a meat grinder for this step). Then finally on to the *lahm b'ajin* bakery, where the baker will transform all of that into delicious, thin *lahm b'ajin*, to eat hot from the oven, with some drops of lemon juice and more hot pepper! In a pure Armenian tradition, large eggplants are cooked in the oven too, and pieces of the soft and melting eggplants are layered on the *lahm b'ajin* and rolled like a sandwich.

To make the dough, dissolve the yeast and sugar in ½ cup (120 ml) lukewarm water and let it proof for 10 minutes. Meanwhile, mix the flour with the vegetable oil and knead well (by hand or machine), adding little by little 1 cup (235 ml) of water. Add the yeast mixture and the salt and continue kneading, adding more water, if necessary (the water quantity will depends on the flour variety), until you obtain a good bread dough. Transfer to a bowl and let it rest for an hour or two until it doubles in volume.

Preheat the oven to 500°F (250°C, or gas mark 10).

All of the topping ingredients must go through a meat grinder fitted with a coarse blade. Mix all the topping ingredients together and pass through the grinder so as to obtain a paste. Do not use an electric mixer or a food processor because it will result in an unsuitable mushy paste.

Cut the dough into walnut-size balls. Sprinkle with flour and roll into very thin disks. Spread the lahm b'ajin mixture over it and bake for about 15 minutes until the beef is cooked and the border turns golden. Serve hot, with few drops of lemon juice and a sprinkle of paprika.

GOOD FRIDAY FOOD

Meat has always been a symbol of wealth and prosperity, consumed on Sundays and at weddings, funerals, and other special events. Fasting periods revolve around food: the time to eat or not and the kind of food to eat or to refrain from. Christians fast from midnight to noon, Muslims from sunrise to sunset.

Fasting periods, such as Christian Lent or Islamic Ramadan, are periods of physical and mental preparation before an important religious and spiritual date (Easter and Eid). While Ramadan does not involve any change in food codes, Christian Lent is very linked to abstaining from meat and often from all meat products called bayyad, or "the whites," such as cheese, butter, and eggs.

Villages have their own traditions of Good Friday food. This is the day when one thinks the least of food, as it is the most sacred day of Lent, and the small amount that has to be eaten on that day has its own codes and meanings. Kebbet el hilleh (the "tricky kibbeh") or kebbeh hazineh (the "sad kibbeh") is the main Good Friday dish. Some regions commemorate this day by cooking with vinegar (which was given to Christ to drink?), or with bitter wild herbs (to represent the bitterness and sadness of the day), or with lentils (to represent Christ's tears).

bulgur chickpea stew

(zenkol)

Yield: 4 servings

---

1 cup (200 g) dried chickpeas

1 cup (160 g) fine-grind bulgur

1 tablespoon (8 g) all-purpose flour

Salt and ground black pepper

2 large yellow onions

4 garlic cloves

2 tablespoons (28 ml) olive oil

½ cup (120 ml) red wine vinegar

What makes a Good Friday dish? In the village and Jezzine and other areas of the South, the answer is this stew. Chickpea-size balls made of a fine bulgur mixture are cooked in an onion and vinegar stew, symbolic of what was given to Christ to drink. Jamileh Nohra prepares *zenkol* like no one else, and she shared her stories and secrets with me.

Soak the chickpeas in water to cover for 10 hours. Drain, place the chickpeas in a large pot, cover with fresh water, and bring to a boil. Lower the heat and simmer until the chickpeas are softened and fully cooked.

Rinse the bulgur in a little water, squeeze well to drain, place in a bowl, and let it rest for an hour. Add the flour, season to taste with salt and pepper, and knead well to form a dough that holds together well (add a few drops of water, if needed). Shape into little balls, each a bit bigger than a chickpea.

Finely chop the onions and garlic. Heat the olive oil in a large skillet over medium heat and sauté the onions and garlic until lightly colored, about 10 minutes. Add to the cooked chickpeas, along with the bulgur balls. Add the vinegar, season to taste with salt, bring to a boil, and simmer for 15 minutes or until the bulgur balls are well cooked. The bulgur balls should swim in a thick sauce. If it is too thin, boil over high heat until the sauce thickens. Serve hot.

homemade noodles with lentils

(reshta)

Yield: 4 servings

————————

1 cup (192 g) lentils

¾ cup + 1 tablespoon (102 g)
   all-purpose flour

Salt

2 large yellow onions

¼ cup (60 ml) olive oil

3 garlic cloves

1 teaspoon dried mint

Juice of 1 lemon

Reshta is the West Beqaa answer for what to serve for Good Friday's lunch: large homemade noodles in a thick lentil stew. Lentils are a Good Friday staple and are said to represent Christ's tears. *Reshta* is a word, and a dish, found in cuisines from central Asia to Iran to the Middle East and even Algeria, where the dish becomes one of vermicelli noodles, which accompanies meat or chicken.

Place the lentils in a large pot, cover with about 2 inches (5 cm) of water, bring to a boil, and then lower the heat and simmer the lentils for 30 minutes. (The water should be over the lentils by a depth of 4 fingers so that there is enough to soak and cook the noodles later on.)

Meanwhile, prepare the noodle dough by mixing the flour in a bowl with just enough water and a pinch of salt to obtain an elastic bread dough. Let it rest, covered, in a warm spot, for 30 minutes.

While the dough rests, finely chop the onions. Heat the olive oil in a large skillet over medium heat and sauté the onions until translucent, about 10 minutes. Add to the cooked lentils.

Roll the dough out into a thin sheet and cut ⅓-inch-wide (1 cm) noodle bands from it. Bring the lentil mixture back to a boil and then drop the noodles into the boiling lentils, one after the other so they do not stick. Let the mixture boil for 10 minutes to cook the noodles.

Crush the garlic and add to the pot, along with the mint and lemon juice. Season to taste with salt. The final consistency of the stew should be neither thin and soupy nor too thick, but somewhere in between. Serve hot.

kibbeh with chickpeas

(kebbet hommos)

Yield: 4 servings

———————

1 cup (200 g) dried chickpeas

2 medium yellow onions

1 cup (160 g) fine-grind bulgur

½ cup (80 g) coarse-grind bulgur

1 cup (125 g) all-purpose flour

½ of a bunch of mint

½ of a bunch of scallions

½ teaspoon ground black pepper

Salt

½ cup (120 ml) vegetable oil

This dish is the town of Zghorta's answer to what to serve for lunch on Good Friday, as well as the town of Ehden, which is part of the same district. These towns are very closely related; most of the residents of Zghorta, a rather coastal town, have homes in Ehden, in the mountains, just below the famous Cedars of Lebanon. They spend winters in Zghorta and summers in Ehden!

Good Friday has a special feel in Zghorta, where everybody dresses in black and mourns Christ's death. And as it is the kibbeh capital, so kibbeh should be eaten on that day too—never with meat, but rather this vegetarian version with chickpeas.

———————————————————————————————

Soak the chickpeas in water to cover for 10 hours. Drain and crush by handfuls in a clean kitchen towel, which will split each chickpea in half and remove the outside peel of the chickpeas. The result is peeled and split chickpeas.

Preheat the oven to 425°F (220°C, or gas mark 7).

Finely grate the onions into a bowl. Add the fine and coarse bulgur and the flour. Finely chop the mint, the scallions, and the split chickpeas and add to the bowl, mixing well. Add the black pepper and season to taste with salt. Knead well, adding a bit of water, if needed, to obtain an elastic dough.

Scoop out walnut-size balls of the kibbeh, shape them into ½-inch-thick (1.3 cm) disks, and arrange in a 12-inch (30 cm) square baking pan. When the pan is all covered in one layer, wet your hand and smooth the surface so that the kibbeh has a uniform thickness. Cut it into triangles so that it does not shrink when cooking and will cook thoroughly. Spread the vegetable oil on top and bake for 45 minutes until it starts browning. Let cool and serve at room temperature.

thick mixed bean soup

(makhlouta)

Yield: 4 servings

———

½ cup (92 g) dried white beans

½ cup (94 g) dried red beans

½ cup (100 g) dried chickpeas

⅓ cup (53 g) coarse-grind bulgur

⅓ cup (64 g) brown lentils

4 medium yellow onions

2 tablespoons (28 ml) olive oil

½ teaspoon ground cumin

Salt

Nothing means mountain rustic food as much as *makhlouta*, or the "mixed," and it is in fact a mix of several kinds of beans and a bit of coarse bulgur, all cooked together in a thick brown porridge-like sauce. *Makhlouta* is a traditional winter dish that needs no excessive spice or seasoning, just the ingredients' pure, rustic flavors. It is also a Lenten dish and often served on Good Friday.

Soak the white beans, red beans, and chickpeas in separate bowls of water to cover for at least 10 hours. Drain the beans, add to a large pot along with fresh water to cover, add the bulgur and the lentils, and bring to a boil. Lower the heat and cook until all the beans are cooked and tender to taste.

Finely chop the onions. Heat the oil in a large skillet over medium heat and sauté the onions until lightly colored. Add the onions to the beans, then add the cumin, season to taste with salt, and cook for 30 more minutes. The consistency of the soup should be porridge-like—not too thick and not too thin. Serve hot.

baked vegetable stew
(masbahet el darwish)

Yield: 4 servings

---

2 medium yellow onions

1 head of garlic

2 tablespoons (28 ml) vegetable oil

1 fresh red or green chile pepper

1 tablespoon (8 g) grated fresh ginger

½ teaspoon 7 spices (page 125)

¼ teaspoon + 1 tablespoon (7 g)
   ground black pepper

Salt

2 carrots

2 medium potatoes

7 ounces (200 g) zucchini

2 medium tomatoes

14 ounces (390 g) cauliflower

7 ounces (200 g) green beans

2 cups (358 g) cooked white
   kidney beans

2 cups (358 g) aïsha khanom
   (or [354 g] cooked red kidney or
   [354 g] borlotti beans)

½ of a bunch of green coriander

1 teaspoon ground coriander

Masbahet el darwish literally means the "dervish's rosary," though I'm not sure why! It is a baked stew of different vegetables, with tomato, beans, and meat. The traditional way to cook it is in a shallow pan in the village bread oven, after the baker finished baking his bread (slow cooking for an hour or two, just in the remaining heat of the oven).

This Good Friday version is obviously meatless and is slowly cooked on a very low fire for hours until all the ingredients meld into a dark brown, thick, syrupy sauce. A main ingredient here is the *aïsha khanom* ("lady aïsha")—the tender version of red beans before they dry and harden (a variety similar to the Italian borlotti beans).

Finely chop the onions and garlic. Heat the vegetable oil in a large skillet over medium heat and sauté the onions and garlic until translucent, about 5 to 10 minutes. Finely chop the chile pepper and add to the onion along with the ginger. Season with the 7 spices, ¼ teaspoon of the black pepper, and salt to taste.

Peel the carrots and the potatoes and cut, along with the zucchini, into thick slices. Peel the tomatoes, if desired, and cut into big chunks. Divide the cauliflower into florets. Cut the green beans into pieces. Season the vegetables with the remaining black pepper and salt to taste.

Start arranging the vegetables in layers in a large pot. Layer one-third of the onion mixture in the bottom of the pan. Divide all the vegetables in half and start layering the first half as follows: a layer of carrots, tomato chunks above it, then potatoes, green beans, zucchini, white beans, and red beans. Then add another one-third of the onion mixture and repeat the same layers of vegetables and beans. End with the cauliflower and the rest of the onion mixture.

Finely chop the green coriander, mix with the ground coriander and ½ cup (120 ml) of water, and drizzle over the vegetables.

Bring to a boil and then lower the heat and cook for 5 hours on a very low fire, checking the water often. All the vegetables will lose water, and you may need to skim off some of the liquid at some point. This dish should not cook with the vegetables covered in water (or else they will boil and be mushy and tasteless), but water should fill half of the pot, and the sauce should reduce to a dark, thick juice at the end.

Let cool in the pot, so the vegetables will cling together better and will be easier to turn out onto a serving plate.

THE SEVEN SPICE MIX

The seven spice mix can be a great mystery. It exists in every Lebanese pantry, but rarely are two alike! The best spice mixes are certainly from Aleppo's souk where the spice tradition has been cultivated for a long time, but you can create your own to your own liking. The traditional version mixes all spice (a staple of Levantine cuisine, what we call *bhhar halou* or sweet pepper), black pepper (giving more heat), cinnamon (another staple), nutmeg, coriander seeds, cloves, and ginger.

SOUK AND STREET FOOD

Oriental souks are somehow ancestors of modern-day malls—Oriental cities used to be walled cities, with quarters dedicated to souks occupied mainly by traders. Each part of the souk is dedicated to one product, or trade: *souk el beharat*, the spice souk; *souk el attarin*, the perfume souk; *souk el qameh*, the wheat (or grain) souk; *souk el dahab*, the gold souk; *souk el khayattin*, the tailors' souk, and so on.

So everybody must be fed, and souk food and drinks must be easy and fast: *foul*, hummus, falafel, *moghrabieh* (Lebanese couscous), coffee, sweets—or rather "sweet" in a singular form, as each sweet maker would specialize in only one kind and master it, rather than doing everything. In the old souk of Tripoli, in northern Lebanon, you can still find the *moghrabieh*

seller with *moghrabieh* sandwiches. (Yes! You should see it to believe it.)

Scenes from a souk must include the fawwal running through the souk with a big tray full of foul (fava beans), hummus, fresh mint, spring onions, olives, and fluorescent pink pickled turnips to be delivered to a shop, and the empty plates and tray to be picked up an hour later. Five-star service! Or the baklava maker, who is white all over from the starch and flour used to roll paper thin multiple layers of baklava dough. Or the neighbor busy for hours stirring a full caldron of halewet el rozz, a Turkish delight–like confection that will be filled with ashta (Arabic cream) and called halewet el rozz (rice sweet) or angels' balls!

eggplant dip

(moutabal)

Yield: 4 servings

────────

2 large eggplants
   (about 2 ¼ pounds, or 1 kg, each)
¼ cup (60 g) tahini
Juice of 2 lemons
1 garlic clove
Salt
Olive oil

Moutabal, otherwise known as baba ghanouj, or France's *caviar d'aubergine* (eggplant caviar), must definitely figure in the top 10 of the best foods in the world! A perfect balance of taste between nutty tahini, smoky eggplant, and a hint of lemon, *moutabal* is the "other" hummus ... just like tabouleh and fattoush, there is hummus and *moutabal*! We always hesitate about which one to serve, but the solution is very simple—just choose both!

Prick the eggplants with a fork on 2 sides. Put them on a medium gas fire (you can put the eggplants directly on a stovetop burner if you have a gas oven, or you can place the eggplants directly on top of a fire in an outdoor grill). The eggplants will blacken on the outside, and the insides will cook in their own moisture to become soft and smoky. Leave the eggplants on the fire until they char on one side (less than 10 minutes) and then turn to the other side to char it. Prick the eggplants with a fork or a knife to be sure they are soft.

Take the eggplants off the fire and let cool for a minute or two (not long, as the charred skin will tint the flesh dark) and then peel off the skin, taking care not to leave small bits of black charred skin. Wash the eggplants well under running water and let drain in a colander.

Squeeze the eggplants well to remove excess water and place in a bowl. Add the tahini and lemon juice and mash all the ingredients together to obtain a purée. Crush the garlic and add to the mixture. Season to taste with salt and store in the fridge for the dip to set. Serve with a generous drizzle of olive oil and the accompaniments of your choice.

hummus

Yield: 4 servings

---

18 ounces (510 g) dried chickpeas

½ cup + 2 tablespoons (150 g) tahini

¾ cup (175 ml) lemon juice
   (around 6 lemons)

Salt

Olive oil

Hummus is the definitive non-home food—even if you find it often in home-cooked meals. A good restaurant is measured by the quality of its hummus, and hummus in the old days used to be bought at the souk *fawwal* only. Hummus is prepared today in special professional machines that very finely grind the cooked chickpeas and other ingredients into a silky smooth paste between steel disks (similar to a stone grain grinder). In the old days, hummus was prepared with a special flat wooden pestle and was crushed and smoothed by hand for nearly an hour!

Home versions today are considered to be good enough made in an electric mixer. The correct proportion of ingredients is always crucial (there should be no overwhelming taste of tahini, garlic, or lemon and there must be a good texture (not runny or too hard), and it must have a fine enough consistency (the chickpeas must be well cooked, and the hummus must run long enough in the mixer). This is a garlic-free version.

Soak the chickpeas in water to cover for 10 hours. Drain, put in a pot, add fresh water to cover and then set to cook over low heat till very tender. Some purists would take off the chickpeas' outer layer or peel after soaking (by crushing the grains in a kitchen towel) and then boil the peeled chickpeas—it makes the end result "finer," they say (I have never tried it, to be honest!). To cook the chickpeas well, the easy way is to add baking soda (1 teaspoon per 1 cup [200 g] chickpeas) to the cooking water. And the other "healthy" way is to replace the baking soda with a 2-inch (5 cm) piece of kombu (Japanese seaweed).

In a food processor, place the chickpeas, tahini, lemon juice, and salt to taste and mix long enough to obtain a smooth, silky paste. A hummus should have the consistency of a dip and not be too thick nor too runny.

Transfer to a bowl, let cool and firm up, and serve with a generous drizzle of olive oil and the accompaniments of your choice.

fava bean stew

(foul medamass)

Yield: 4 servings

———————

¾ cup (120 g) dried small brown fava beans

1 medium yellow onion, peeled and halved

2 garlic cloves, peeled

Handful of split yellow lentils (dal)

1 lemon plus the juice of 2 lemons

⅓ cup (80 ml) olive oil

Ground cumin

Salt

Foul means "fava beans" and is the name of the green fava (*foul akhdar*), the dried beans, and the dish itself. *Foul medamass* (seasoned fava) is somewhere between a salad and a stew. It must be very well cooked, until mushy, then seasoned like a salad, served hot, and eaten with bread, onion, mint, and tomato.

Foul is the ultimate souk food. You would often see the *fawwal* (foul maker) running in the narrow alleys with a tray full of bowls—one of *foul* and others containing crisp white onions, mint, tomato, radishes, olives, and bread. A perfect meal!

This recipe is from Azza Fahmi, a wonderful jewelry designer who brings ancient Islamic motifs into modern jewelry. The fava beans used here must be brown, round, and small, not the greenish, flat, large beans.

———————————————————

Soak the fava beans in water to cover for 10 hours. Drain and put in a pot. Add the onion halves, the whole garlic cloves, and the lentils. Add enough fresh water to cover by 2 fingers, bring to a boil, and skim the foam that will form at the top. Then lower the heat as much as possible and cook until the beans are very well cooked and mushy. This will take several hours. (Azza has an electric hot plate with a very low temperature, where she leaves her foul to cook overnight.)

When cooked, cut the whole lemon into quarters and add to the pot and let cook for a further 20 minutes. Take off the heat, add the lemon juice, olive oil, cumin, and salt to taste, and serve hot. It can also be served with a handful of cooked whole chickpeas tossed into it.

chickpeas with yogurt

(fatteh hommos)

Yield: 4 servings

———

1 cup (200 g) dried chickpeas

1 garlic clove

Salt

1 ¼ cups (290 g) yogurt

2 tablespoons (30 g) tahini

1 tablespoon (15 ml) olive oil

2 pitas

5 ½ tablespoons (50 g) pine nuts

1 teaspoon vegetable oil

Fatteh is typical souk food, mainly of the souks of Damascus. Already prepared ingredients are mixed at the last minute and served immediately—cooked chickpeas, yogurt, grilled bread, and traditionally browned butter or ghee drizzled on top. A fatteh must be served and eaten quickly, before the grilled bread gets soggy from the yogurt.

A fatteh is a perfect balance between the hot chickpeas and the cold yogurt. The yogurt is not served plain, but "broken" with tahini and a hint of garlic. I like to add a bit of olive oil to the yogurt, which rounds out the flavors even further.

———

Soak the chickpeas in water to cover for 10 hours. Drain, put in a pot with fresh water to cover, and simmer over low heat until well cooked.

Meanwhile, crush the garlic finely with a bit of salt. Add to the yogurt and tahini in a bowl, mix well, and then add the olive oil and blend. Grill the pitas on a stovetop griddle or toast it in the oven until crisp and golden.

In a small skillet over medium heat, sauté the pine nuts in the vegetable oil, stirring constantly, until lightly colored.

Divide the quantities among 4 bowls. Start with the cooked chickpeas (and a bit of their cooking water), add the yogurt sauce, and top with the grilled bread, broken into pieces. Top with the pine nuts and serve immediately.

falafel

There is always space to argue about variations on dishes, and so it is true with falafel too! Where is it from? Where is the best one? How should it be made? I'll stop on this last issue!

Of course, two camps exist: the fava-only falafel camp and those who preach the combination of favas and chickpeas. Then again, there are also those who swear by coriander versus those who swear by parsley! There are no rules, only different variations around one theme. And it's for each to choose his or her favorite.

Here is one of the many versions! Still, the secret of any good falafel is to eat it hot enough to be golden and crispy on the outside and tender and moist on the inside. Another secret is to eat it in a sandwich because a falafel is not just about a deep-fried ball of something, but rather about the mix and contrast of the fried falafel with the tarator (tahini sauce), juicy tomato, fragrant mint, crisp parsley, crunchy radish, and pickled chile pepper, all in one bite with some flatbread!

Yield: 4 servings

---

1 cup (160 g) fava beans
    (large, pale green, split,
    and skinned)
½ cup (100 g) dried chickpeas
1 medium yellow onion
2 garlic cloves, peeled
1 bunch of green coriander
1 teaspoon baking powder
1 teaspoon ground cumin
1 teaspoon ground coriander
½ teaspoon ground ginger
Salt
Vegetable oil, for frying
Tahini Sauce (page 136),
    for serving

Soak the fava beans and the chickpeas in separate bowls with water to cover for 10 hours. Drain and mix together in a bowl.

Cut the onion into eighths and add to the bowl. Add the garlic cloves, green coriander, baking powder, cumin, ground coriander, and ginger and season to taste with salt.

In a food processor, whiz small batches of this mixture to obtain a paste. The consistency of the falafel depends on this paste, which must not be too smooth (so as not to have soggy falafel) nor too coarse (so as not to have crumbling ones). Knead the paste by hand a little longer, if needed, to make sure it will hold together, adding 1 tablespoon (8 g) of flour, if necessary.

To shape the falafel, there is a falafel shaper that quickly creates balls. If that is not available, use a small utensil such as an ice-cream scoop to portion walnut-size balls of the falafel mix. In fact, falafel are not shaped as balls in the end, but as thick disks—it is important to obtain falafel that are not so thin that they will dry when fried, but are thick enough to crisp on the outside and stay moist from the inside. Flatten the balls a bit into disks.

Heat vegetable oil in a deep pot over medium heat or a deep fryer. Deep-fry the falafel disk until golden and crisp on both sides. Serve the falafel hot, with the tahini sauce.

tahini sauce
(tarator)

Yield: 1 cup (235 ml)

---

1 garlic clove

Salt

1 cup (240 g) tahini

Juice of 3 lemons

1 tablespoon (15 ml) olive oil

Tarator is not a dish, but rather a very versatile sauce. It is the traditional sauce for falafel and shawarma and also goes well with baked fish, deep-fried cauliflower (see page 83), or simple boiled potatoes (with a bit of parsley on top).

Tahini is sesame paste. Nowadays, health food concerns have brought back to the market a type of tahini made from whole sesame seeds, which is slightly darker and nuttier in taste than tahini made from hulled sesame seeds and definitely a better choice. A few drops of olive oil in the tarator always lend a rounder note to the sauce.

Crush the garlic together with a bit of salt, add to the tahini in a bowl, and add the lemon juice. When the lemon juice is added, the tahini will react and thicken, so just continue stirring to smooth it out and add more lemon juice, if needed. You will know when you have the correct amount of lemon juice because the mixture will have a smooth consistency. Season to taste with salt, blend in olive oil, and serve.

garlic paste
(toum)

Yield: 1 cup (235 ml)

————

4 garlic cloves, peeled
1 egg white
1 cup (235 ml) vegetable oil
Salt
1 teaspoon lemon juice

Toum is a garlic sauce, or, more accurately, a garlic cream. Not very attractive to vampires and the garlic haters out there, but it is an exquisite, smooth, silky garlic cream that fast becomes an addiction. *Toum* goes with grilled chicken, is divine with French fries, and beautifully accompanies *malssa*, puréed raw meat.

Toum comes in many versions, but is basically finely crushed garlic and oil (preferably vegetable oil, not olive oil, as the latter is too strong in flavor and color) worked together like a mayonnaise to obtain a light, airy cream. To make it lighter and easier, you can add an egg white, in the style of mayonnaise.

My mother's Sunday exercise used to be making *toum* for the barbecued chicken, crushing and stirring for a long time to transform the garlic and oil into a creamy paste. The easy alternative today is to let an electric mixer do the job.

————————————————

In an electric mixer, whiz together the garlic and the egg white, adding the vegetable oil in a very thin drizzle. The oil must not be added too fast or it will not incorporate into the mixture. Toum will form quickly into a white cream. Season to taste with salt and add the lemon juice, which will make the white color brighter.

fried eggplant with yogurt and pine nuts

(fatteh batenjenn)

Another take on the fatteh is this one, with deep-fried eggplant. *Fatteh hommos* is about the contrast between the boiled chickpeas, grilled bread, and smooth yogurt. The textures are similar for this dish; the contrast is more about the different flavors than the textures.

Yield: 4 servings

————

2 large eggplants
   (about 2 ¼ pounds, or 1 kg, each)
Salt
¼ cup (31 g) all-purpose flour
Vegetable oil
2 pitas
5 ½ tablespoons (50 g) pine nuts
2 garlic cloves
1 ¾ cups (410 g) yogurt

Cut the eggplant into slices, sprinkle generously with salt, and leave in a colander to drain for 10 hours to remove excess water. Dry with paper towels and cut the slices into cubes. Sprinkle with the flour and then shake well to remove excess flour and keep just a thin coat of flour on the eggplant cubes.

Heat vegetable oil in a deep pot over medium heat or a deep fryer. Deep-fry the eggplant cubes until crispy and golden. Drain on paper towels. Grill the pitas on a stovetop griddle or in a hot oven until golden and crispy. Break into pieces.

In a small skillet over medium heat, sauté the pine nuts in 2 tablespoons (28 ml) vegetable oil, stirring constantly, until golden.

Crush the garlic with a bit of salt and combine with the yogurt.

Serve either in a big bowl or as individual servings. Start with a layer of deep-fried eggplant, topped generously with the yogurt, and then topped with the broken grilled bread and pine nuts.

SWEETS

Middle Eastern sweets have a reputation for being honeyed, sticky sweets, but this is far from reality. The sticky baklava you may know is rather a bad Occidental version, far away from the real thing of multiple paper-thin layers of crispy pastry.

Sweets too, come in two versions: souk sweets and home sweets. Souk sweets are elaborate in their techniques, cooking, and ingredients. In the old souk, a baklawa maa'lem (master) would make only baklawa, knowing how to roll out 20 thin layers of starched white dough together to obtain a light andv crispy baklawa.

Home sweets are easier to prepare and more affordable in terms of ingredients, utensils, and techniques.

The desserts in this chapter are made with no eggs, butter, or animal products.

carob cake

(sfouf b' debs)

Yield: 4 to 8 servings

———————

2 tablespoons (14 g) whole aniseed

2 cups (250 g) all-purpose flour

1 cup (235 ml) vegetable oil

1 cup (320 g) carob molasses

1 tablespoon (14 g) baking powder

1 tablespoon (15 g) tahini

2 tablespoons (16 g) sesame seeds

Sfouf is a simple butter-free, egg-free cake made from flour and carob molasses. Simple and healthy, it's the definitive mountain sweet.

Carob has found new converts recently in health food shops as an alternative to chocolate. In the Lebanese mountains, it has never been an alternative, but always the "real thing." Carob is a wild tree that grows in middle altitudes and produces dark brown pods that hold a thick liquid (extracted by pressing) that is carob molasses. An important part of the *mouneh*, the winter preserves, carob molasses is mainly eaten mixed with tahini (to create our local chocolate spread) or used as a syrup or sweetener for desserts.

My mother's recipe for carob cake is "to the eye"—deciding the quantities by the eye (that is, 5 cups [625 g] of flour, 1 cup [235 ml] of vegetable oil, 1 tablespoon [14 g] of baking powder, and then enough carob molasses to obtain the right consistency of a cake mix). Here, for your ease, is a recipe from my friend, Tamar, who works in measurements!

Preheat the oven to 350°F (180°C, or gas mark 4).

Bring 1 ½ cups (355 ml) of water to a boil in a small pot. Boil the aniseed for 1 minute and then let it cool. Strain the water and discard the aniseed.

Rub by hand the flour with the vegetable oil in a large bowl so all the grains get coated with oil. Add just 1 cup (235 ml) of the strained aniseed water, the carob molasses, and the baking powder and whisk to obtain a smooth batter.

Use a 10-inch (25.4 cm) diameter round cake pan (or similar in size, rectangular or square) and instead of buttering it, spread the tahini all inside so the sfouf won't stick. Pour in the batter, even it out, and sprinkle uniformly with the sesame seeds.

Bake for 50 minutes or as long as needed to cook through (check it with a cake tester, which should come out clean). Let it cool on a rack and then cut into pieces and serve at room temperature. Sfouf keeps for more than a week in an airtight container.

turmeric cake

(sfouf)

Here is another version of *sfouf*, sweetened with granulated sugar and colored and spiced with turmeric. It's a very simple dessert to prepare that just needs mixing by hand.

Yield: 4 to 8 servings

3 cups (375 g) all-purpose flour

½ cup (120 ml) vegetable oil

1 cup (200 g) sugar

1 tablespoon (7 g) ground turmeric

1 cup (235 ml) milk

1 tablespoon (15 g) tahini

⅓ cup (31 g) blanched
   halved almonds

Preheat the oven to 350°F (180°C, or gas mark 4).

Rub by hand the flour with the vegetable oil in a large bowl so all the grains get coated with oil. Dissolve the sugar and turmeric in the milk, then add it to the flour, and whisk to obtain a smooth batter.

Use a 10-inch (25.4 cm) diameter round cake pan (or similar in size, rectangular or square) and instead of buttering it, spread the tahini all over the inside so the cake won't stick. Pour the batter into it, even it out, and disperse the almonds evenly on top.

Bake for 50 minutes or as long as needed to cook it through (check it with a cake tester, which should come out clean). Let it cool on a rack and then cut into pieces and serve at room temperature. Sfouf keeps for more than a week in an airtight container.

chilled apricot soup

(khoshaf)

Damascus is known for its apricots, which are preserved as dried fruits or as *ammaredin*, thick apricot paste dried in sheets, which must be soaked and diluted in water to make the *khoshaf*. *Khoshaf* is a thick, sweet cold soup made from these dried apricots and seasoned with all kinds of dried fruits, nuts, and seeds; it's like *1001 Nights* turned into a dessert!

Yield: 4 servings

———

1 sheet ammaredin (or 18 ounces [510 g] dried apricots)

⅓ cup (48 g) almonds

3 ½ tablespoons (28 g) shelled pistachios

5 ½ tablespoons (50 g) pine nuts

¼ cup (50 g) sugar

1 tablespoon (15 ml) orange blossom water

1 teaspoon rose water

4 ½ tablespoons (50 g) prunes, chopped

⅓ cup (50 g) raisins

Scant ½ cup (65 g) dried apricots, chopped

Cut the ammaredinn (or dried apricots) into small pieces and soak in 2 cups (475 ml) water for 10 hours. If all the pieces have not yet dissolved after that time (or if you are using dried apricots), whiz the mixture for a minute in a blender to obtain a smooth, lump-free apricot soup.

Soak the almonds, pistachios, and pine nuts in separate bowls of water to cover for 2 hours. Drain and peel the skins from the almonds and the pistachios (rubbing them in a clean kitchen towel will help).

Add the nuts to the apricot soup, along with the sugar, orange blossom water, rose water, chopped prunes, raisins, and chopped apricots. Mix well and chill until ready to serve. Serve cold.

fried biscuits in scented syrup

(maakroun)

Yield: About 60 biscuits

For the biscuits:

1 ¼ cups + 2 ½ tablespoons (325 ml) vegetable oil

8 cups (1 kg) all-purpose flour

6 ½ cups (488 g) semolina flour

1 tablespoon (7 g) whole aniseed

For the syrup:

2 ½ cups (500 g) sugar

1 cup (235 ml) water

3 unsprayed leaves of scented geranium (optional)

2 tablespoons (28 ml) orange blossom water

Juice of 1 lemon

Vegetable oil, for frying

Fried sweets are a staple of party days, when village squares are filled with cauldrons of boiling frying oil producing a variety of fried treats. Fried sweets are a post-Christmas tradition, too, when in the old times "frying nights" were between Christmas and Epiphany (January 6) and a pot of boiling oil was always on in the kitchen to produce *maakroun, zlebyieh* (fried bread sticks), and *ouwaymet* (fried dough balls).

Maakroun are finger-like biscuits that are fried and then dipped while hot into a syrup that is scented with the garden's herbs, mainly *ooter*, the scented geranium.

To make the biscuits, warm the vegetable oil and rub it into the all-purpose and semolina flours to coat the grains of flour.

Bring 2 cups (475 ml) water to a boil and boil the aniseed for about 4 minutes. Strain the water and discard the aniseed. Add the aniseed water to the flour mixture, little by little, kneading well to obtain a dough similar to a bread dough. You may not need all the water, as the water quantity will depend on the flour's quality. Let the dough rest, covered, for 1 hour.

Meanwhile, prepare the syrup by boiling the sugar, water, and geranium leaves for 5 minutes in a pot. Add the orange blossom water and lemon juice at the last minute. (If geranium leaves are not available, the orange blossom water is enough to scent the syrup.)

To shape the biscuits, take a small piece of dough and roll it thin into the size and shape of an average finger. To imprint a traditional pattern on the dough, hold the piece of dough with 3 fingers and roll it over the surface of a large colander or a basket. Repeat until all the dough is used.

Heat vegetable oil in a deep pot over medium heat or in a deep fryer. Deep-fry the biscuits in batches in the hot oil until golden all over, and, as they are done, transfer them immediately from the fryer to the syrup. Let the biscuits soak for 30 seconds and then transfer to a rack to drain. Serve at room temperature.

wheat, fruits, and nuts

(qamhyieh)

Yield: 4 servings

———

3 cups (576 g) wheat berries

⅓ cup (48 g) almonds

3 ½ tablespoons (28 g) shelled
  pistachios

5 ½ tablespoons (50 g) pine nuts

½ cup (50 g) walnuts

6 tablespoons (78 g) sugar

1 tablespoon (15 ml) orange
  blossom water

⅓ cup (50 g) raisins

¼ cup (44 g) pomegranate arils

Qamhyieh means "wheaty" and is simply boiled wheat mixed with dried fruits and nuts, sweetened with sugar, and scented with orange blossom water. You could say it's our local take on granola!

  Qamhyieh is our Barbara sweet, the local Halloween, on December 4, that commemorates Santa Barbara, a fervent Christian who lived in Baalbeck, says the myth, and was running away from her father, a pagan general of the Roman army, when a bare field miraculously grew with tall wheat where she could hide. *Qamhyieh* is also traditionally made when a baby's first tooth appears, to be shared with family, neighbors, and guests.

———

Bring a pot of water to a boil and add the wheat berries. The water should cover the wheat berries by 2 fingers. Lower the heat, cover, and cook the wheat berries until soft. This may take up to 2 hours. When cooked, the cooking water should be thick and have a gravy-like consistency. If this is not the case, raise the heat and boil uncovered.

Meanwhile, soak the almonds, pistachios, pine nuts, and walnuts separately in bowls of water to cover for 2 hours. Drain and peel the almonds, pistachios, and walnuts (rubbing them in a clean kitchen towel will help).

Add the sugar to the warm cooked wheat and stir well. Then add the orange blossom water, all of the nuts, and the raisins. Finish by topping with the pomegranate arils. Serve immediately.

sesame bars

(semsemyieh)

Semsemyieh is a typical souk dessert, made of toasted sesame seeds and ground almonds set in a sweet syrup, though it could also be made from chopped cashews, or all almonds, or pistachios. Large blocks of the candy are prepared and cut into bite-size pieces for serving.

Yield: About 20 pieces

---

2 ¼ pounds (1 kg) sesame seeds

1 ⅓ cups (193 g) almonds

1 cup (200 g) sugar

½ cup + 2 tablespoons (200 g) honey

2 tablespoons (30 g) tahini

Toast the sesame seeds in a dry skillet, stirring constantly, until the seeds are uniformly golden. In a food processor, whiz the almonds to a fine powder.

Mix the sugar and the honey in a pot and boil to obtain a thick syrup. Add the almond powder and stir well. Add the toasted sesame seeds and mix well.

Spread the tahini on the bottom and sides of a 12-inch (30 cm) square baking pan. Spread the hot sesame mixture thinly in the pan (it should be less than ⅓ inch [1 cm] thick). Wet your hand and even out the surface. Let cool and set.

Refrigerate the pan for 4 hours for the candy to set well and harden and then cut into bite-size pieces. It will keep for about a month if kept in an airtight container in the refrigerator.

rice pudding with spices

(meghli)

Yield: 10 servings

½ cup (80 g) rice flour

½ cup (100 g) sugar

1 tablespoon (6 g) ground caraway

1 tablespoon (7 g) ground cinnamon

2 tablespoons (12 g) ground aniseed

5 ⅓ tablespoons (48 g) pine nuts

3 ½ tablespoons (28 g) shelled
  pistachios

⅓ cup (48 g) almonds

Meghli is the "newborn" sweet. Whenever a mother gives birth, *meghli* is the first thing to prepare at home to offer to family and guests. And since Christmas is about a newborn, too, *meghli* is served as a Christmas dessert in the mountains.

Meghli is a fragrant brown rice pudding, sweetened with sugar; seasoned with anise, caraway, and cinnamon; and topped with almonds and pistachios. The legend goes that the brown *meghli* is a symbol of a fertile soil, with seeds on top of it that will sprout into life!

Meghli means "boiled," and so the secret here is to boil this pudding for the longest time possible, over low heat, to acquire a thick consistency.

Bring a pot with 6 cups (1.4 L) water to a boil. Dissolve the rice flour, sugar, caraway, cinnamon, and aniseed in 1 cup (235 ml) water and add this mixture to the boiling water, stirring constantly so that the rice powder does not form lumps. Lower the heat and continue stirring for the rice to cook and the pudding to acquire a thick consistency, about 1 hour.

Pour into individual serving bowls and let it cool and set. Transfer to the refrigerator to chill.

While the pudding chills, soak the pine nuts, pistachios, and almonds separately in bowls of water to cover for around 2 hours. Drain and peel the skins from the pistachios and almonds (rubbing them in a clean kitchen towel will help). Serve the pudding with the mixed nuts sprinkled on top.

INDEX

INDEX

INDEX

INDEX

ACKNOWLEDGMENTS

This is not my book, this is a woman's book. Start with a mother, an aunt, family, neighbors, the nun cook of the neighboring convent, friends: any of those wonderful individuals who all think they make the best tabouleh and maamoul, and who pass on their history and tradition through the daily ritual of cooking and eating, through keshek, jams, pickles, and mehsheh.

For the women who come to Souk el Tayeb and Tawlet, who are always proud of who they are and what they do, for their kebbeh and tabouleh. Those who live by the phrase "make food, not war."

Thank you, moms!

ABOUT THE AUTHOR

Kamal Mouzawak is the founder of Souk el Tayeb, Lebanon's first farmers market, and of the farmer's kitchen Tawlet. A son of farmers and producers, Kamal grew up in gardens and kitchens, tasting life, food, and land fruits at their source.

After studying graphic design, Kamal followed paths of food and travel writing, as a macrobiotic cooking teacher, and as a healthy cooking television chef. This all lead to more involvement with social and environmental change and transformation.

Since its first days in 2004, Souk el Tayeb had the vision of celebrating food and traditions that unite communities while promoting small-scale farmers and producers, as well as the culture of sustainable agriculture. Today, Souk el Tayeb is an institution that includes a weekly farmers market, "food & feast" regional festivals, "souk @ school" education and awareness programs, el tayeb newsletter, "dekenet Souk el tayeb", and the latest project of "tawlet Souk el Tayeb," the farmers' kitchen.

NOUVEAUTES SEVAN وقوتيه سيڤان

KOKO ՆՈՐՈՅԹՆԵՐ ՍԵՒԱՆ